P9-DZX-986

Systematic Thinking for Social Action

THE H. ROWAN GAITHER LECTURES
IN SYSTEMS SCIENCE

are named in memory of one of the founders
and the first Chairman of the Board of the RAND Corporation.
They were established by gift of the System Development Corporation,
formerly a division of the RAND Corporation,
and are arranged by the Graduate School of Business Administration
and the Center for Research in Management Science
of the University of California, Berkeley.
Charles J. Hitch was the first lecturer in the series.
Charles L. Schultze was the second.
Alice M. Rivlin was the third.

ALICE M. RIVLIN

Systematic Thinking for Social Action

H. Rowan Gaither Lectures, delivered January 1970, at the University of California, Berkeley, under the sponsorship of the Graduate School of Business Administration and the Center for Research in Management Science

THE BROOKINGS INSTITUTION *Washington, D.C.*

THE BROOKINGS INSTITUTION
1775 Massachusetts Avenue, N.W., Washington, D.C. 20036

ISBN 0-8157-7478-8 (cloth)
ISBN 0-8157-7477-x (paper)

Library of Congress Catalog Card Number 74-161600

9 8 7 6 5 4 3 2

THE BROOKINGS INSTITUTION is an independent organization devoted to nonpartisan research, education, and publication in economics, government, foreign policy, and the social sciences generally. Its principal purposes are to aid in the development of sound public policies and to promote public understanding of issues of national importance.

The Institution was found on December 8, 1927, to merge the activities of the Institute for Government Research, founded in 1916, the Institute of Economics, founded in 1922, and the Robert Brookings Graduate School of Economics and Government, founded in 1924.

The general administration of the Institution is the responsibility of a Board of Trustees charged with maintaining the independence of the staff and fostering the most favorable conditions for creative research and education. The immediate direction of the policies, program, and staff of the Institution is vested in the President, assisted by an advisory committee of the officers and staff.

In publishing a study, the Institution presents it as a competent treatment of a subject worthy of public consideration. The interpretations and conclusions in such publications are those of the author or authors and do not necessarily reflect the views of the other staff members, officers, or trustees of the Brookings Institution.

Foreword

In recent years, Americans have devoted a growing share of their national resources to public programs for meeting social needs. Funds for education, health services, manpower training, income maintenance, and related programs are expanding rapidly in state, local, and federal budgets. Yet, dissatisfaction with these programs has never been more widespread. Public aspirations for more social services and more effective social services have risen at least as fact as funds expended.

Responding to these demands, economists and other social scientists have turned their attention to measuring social needs, evaluating the effectiveness of government programs to meet them, and estimating the costs and benefits of alternative programs. How successful has the effort been? In this book, Alice M. Rivlin attempts to evaluate the evaluators—to give a "midterm report card" on the progress of the analysts in improving the basis for public decisions on social action programs.

The grades are mixed. The author finds that there has been considerable progress in identifying social problems and estimating who would gain if social programs were successful. But little progress has been made in comparing the benefits of different social programs—the analysts cannot say whether another million dollars would be better spent to cure cancer or to teach children to read. Far more serious, little progress has been made in distinguishing more effective from less effective approaches even to well-defined social ends. The author maintains that education, health, and welfare systems are not organized so as to provide information on the effectiveness of alternative ways of delivering these services. We are not likely to discover more effective ways until we conduct systematic experiments with different ways of delivering social services and analyze the results.

Mrs. Rivlin is an economist and a senior fellow of the Brookings Institution. She has served in government—most recently in the Department of Health, Education, and Welfare, where she was Assistant Secretary for Planning and Evaluation. Her book is based on the H. Rowan Gaither Lectures in Systems Science delivered at the University of California in January 1970.

The author is deeply indebted to many colleagues and associates who shared their ideas and made helpful suggestions on the manuscript. She is particularly grateful to C. Worth Bateman, William Gorham, Rashi Fein, Guy H. Orcutt, Thomas I. Ribich, Heather Ross, Jeffrey H. Weiss, William B. Ross, Walter Williams, Joseph A. Pechman, Charles L. Schultze, Henry J. Aaron, and Robert W. Hartman. She is also indebted to Mary S. vonEuler for research assistance, to Mendelle T. Berenson for editing the manuscript, to Evelyn P. Fisher for checking its accuracy, and to Joan C. Culver for preparing the index.

The views expressed in this book are those of the author. They do not necessarily reflect the views of the trustees, the officers, or other staff members of the Brookings Institution.

KERMIT GORDON
President

April 1971
Washington, D.C.

Contents

1 Introduction 1

PPBS and Common Sense 3
A Word about PPBS in HEW 5
Four Propositions 6

2 Who Wins and Who Loses? 9

What Are the Problems? 9
Income Maintenance 16
The "Tax Model" 35
Higher Education 36

3 What Does the Most Good? 46

Identifying the Objectives 46
Comparing the Benefits: Cancer Cure versus Reading 51
Weakness of Benefit-Cost Analysis 56
When Benefit-Cost Analysis Is Useful 60

4 Producing Effective Services: What Do We Know? 64

Why Do We Care? 65
Learning from the System 69
Learning from Federal Programs 79

5 Can We Find Out What Works? 86

Random Innovation 87
Systematic Experimentation 91
The Pros and Cons of an Experimental Strategy 108

6 Accountability: What Does It Mean? 120

Decentralization 122
Community Control 130
The Market Model 133
Where Do We Go from Here? 140

Index 145

1 Introduction

The Gaither Lectures, by an unbroken if brief tradition, address the question: How can government make decisions in a more rational way? To care about this question one has to have faith in the ability of nations to solve at least some of their problems by collective action. One also has to have sufficient faith in rationality to believe that analysis of a problem generally leads to a better decision. H. Rowan Gaither believed in governments, rationality, and the ability of people trained in systematic analysis to improve government decision making. Those who have delivered these lectures in his honor share that faith.

Charles Hitch focused the first series of Gaither Lectures on the problem of making better decisions about the national defense.[1] He recounted the history of the fragmented United States defense establishment and showed the importance of central control for the effective use of defense resources. He described the reorganization and the tools through which control was to be achieved—the planning-programming-budgeting system (PPBS) introduced into the Department of Defense in 1961.

Charles Schultze, in the second series of Gaither Lectures, widened the discussion to include the whole domestic side of the federal government.[2] He contrasted PPBS with an alternative decision-making model, which he called, after Lindblom, "muddling through,"[3] and, analyzing the politics of decision making, demonstrated how the system is compatible with a democratic political process.

Both Hitch and Schultze argued cogently that government

1. Charles J. Hitch, *Decision-Making for Defense* (University of California Press, 1965).

2. Charles L. Schultze, *The Politics and Economics of Public Spending* (Brookings Institution, 1968).

3. Charles E. Lindblom, "The Science of 'Muddling Through,' " *Public Administration Review*, Vol. 19 (Spring 1959), pp. 79–88.

should make decisions as systematically as possible—arraying alternative policies, assembling information on the advantages and disadvantages of each, and estimating the costs and benefits of public action. From their analyses of such tools of systematic decision making as program budgets, multiyear plans, and program memoranda, two major messages come through: (1) It is better to have some idea where you are going than to fly blind; and (2) it is better to be orderly than haphazard about decision making.

Neither Hitch nor Schultze, however, overstated the case for system or analysis. Both recognized the important role of judgment and values in the decision-making process. As Hitch put it, "Systems analysis is simply a method to get before the decision-maker the relevant data, organized in a way most useful to him."[4]

This third series of lectures will continue this discussion of how to make government decisions more rationally, but will change the focus in two ways. First, its emphasis will be on a particular set of what I call "social action" programs—education, health, manpower training, and income maintenance and various other efforts to alleviate poverty. These are human investment, or "people," programs, designed to help individuals function better, that at the federal level fall under the jurisdiction of the Department of Health, Education, and Welfare, the Office of Economic Opportunity, and parts of the Department of Labor.

Second, I will concentrate on the substance, not the process, of decision making. No purpose would be served by a reexamination of PPBS or reiteration of the case for systematic analysis of social action programs. That case has been ably made and widely accepted. By now the analysts have been on

4. Hitch, *Decision-Making for Defense*, p. 53.

the scene for several years and it is time to evaluate their contribution. With what kinds of decisions have they proved helpful? Where have they been unable to help? What should be done to make systematic analysis more useful? These lectures will attempt to give a midterm report card on the contributions of analysis to decisions concerning social action.

PPBS and Common Sense

Despite its elaborate terminology, PPBS seems to me simply a commonsense approach to decision making. Anyone faced with the problem of running a government program, or, indeed, any large organization, would want to take these steps to assure a good job: (1) Define the objectives of the organization as clearly as possible; (2) find out what the money was being spent for and what was being accomplished; (3) define alternative policies for the future and collect as much information as possible about what each would cost and what it would do; (4) set up a systematic procedure for bringing the relevant information together at the time the decisions were to be made. PPBS was simply an attempt to institutionalize this commonsense approach in the government budgeting process. It was not the first such attempt and it will not be the last.

The tools and the terminology may change, but the approach to decision making implicit in PPBS has largely, I think, been accepted in Washington, in principle if not always in practice. It is regarded as a desirable way to make decisions—if the time and information are available. Hardly anyone explicitly favors a return to muddling through.

Indeed, PPBS is only one manifestation of a quiet revolution in the government in the last few years: The level of discussion of major decisions has gone up. The result is reflected in the questions decision makers ask about new programs, as well as those already in effect. What will it do? Why do we need it? What does it cost? They do not get very good answers yet, but they keep asking, and the standards of staff work are rising. The quiet revolution is also reflected in the acceptance of analysis as part of the decision process and of the analyst as a participant at the decision table. No one demands of the analyst, "Why are you here?" Now they ask, "What have you got to contribute?" Sometimes he has a lot to say and sometimes he is very quiet.

In the process, the mystique has gone out of planning and systems analysis. The practitioners themselves, in fact, never invoked as much mystique as the nonpractitioners alleged. Moreover, a touch of mystique was probably useful. A bit of bravado is necessary to overcome the inertia of government, to get attention, and to win a place at the decision table. Now, however, educators, doctors, and ordinary civil servants realize that systems analysts do not have pointy heads, that they can be helpful and sometimes even right. The analysts in turn have recognized that educators, doctors, civil servants—even generals—are knowledgeable, necessary, and not always wrong.

Moreover, the tools of the trade have become more familiar and thus less frightening. As recently as five or six years ago the average administrator viewed computers as somewhat menacing new instruments. In his Gaither Lectures, Hitch felt called upon to say, "Let it be said, here and now, that computers do not make decisions . . ."[5] That is certainly correct, but it already sounds dated. Decision makers no longer need to be reassured that they are not about to be put out of business by a computer.

The cockiness of systems analysts has disappeared with the

5. Hitch, *Decision-Making for Defense*, p. 76.

mystique. If any analyst thought it was going to be easy to make social action programs work better or to make more rational choices among programs, he is by now a sadder and a wiser man. The choices are genuinely hard and the problems are extraordinarily complex and difficult. It is hard to design an income maintenance system that will both assure adequate incomes to the needy and encourage people to work, or a health financing system that will both assure proper care to the sick and encourage efficient use of health resources. It is hard to decide how the government should allocate its resources among different kinds of social action programs. So far the analysts have probably done more to reveal how difficult the problems and choices are than to make the decisions easier.

A Word about PPBS in HEW

These lectures will not evaluate PPBS as a set of procedures, but a word about the role of PPBS in government decision making is perhaps in order. In the Department of Health, Education, and Welfare, its most important effect was the creation of an analytical staff at the department level, which brought into the secretary's office a group of people who were trained to think analytically and whose job it was to improve the process of decision making.[6] Although I am not an unbiased judge, I think the small planning and evaluation staff in HEW has accomplished an astonishing amount since it was created in late 1965. It has developed a program budget and information

6. I have discussed these activities at greater length in "The Planning, Programming, and Budgeting System in the Department of Health, Education, and Welfare: Some Lessons from Experience," in *The Analysis and Evaluation of Public Expenditures: The PPB System*, A Compendium of Papers submitted to the Subcommittee on Economy in Government of the Joint Economic Committee, Vol. 3, Pt. 5, 91 Cong. 1 sess. (1969), pp. 909–22.

system that, while far from perfect, gives the secretary a better idea of how department funds are being spent, of what they are buying and for whom. It has started evaluation studies to try to measure the impact of departmental programs. The five-year plan for the department it has developed and periodically revised forces a lot of people to think harder about the objectives of programs and their future directions. It has produced analytical work that has had considerable impact on major policy choices. Finally, but perhaps most important, it has helped create a regular process for bringing analysis to bear on budgetary and legislative decisions, and it has established the voice of the analysts and planners in the decision process. (The voice is important; decision makers rarely have time to read!) Indeed, some of the procedural steps taken in the department under the impetus of PPBS seem so obviously useful that it is hard to remember that they are so new.

But now the process exists. Missionaries need no longer be sent to convert the heathen to the virtues of systematic analysis. If the analysts have something relevant and useful to say they will be listened to. Now that they have the floor, what do they have to say?

Four Propositions

Anyone who makes decisions about social action programs—a congressman, the Secretary of HEW, the Governor of Nebraska, or a concerned voter—would want answers to such questions as these:

1. How do we define the problems, and how are they distributed? Who is poor or sick or inadequately educated?

2. Who would be helped by specific social action programs, and how much?

3. What would do the most good? How do the benefits of different kinds of programs compare?

4. How can particular kinds of social services be produced most effectively?

In the last few years, economists, statisticians, and other analysts have worked on all of these sets of problems, with results that are highly uneven. Four propositions, two positive and two negative, sum up the progress so far. Chapter 2 discusses the first two.

The first proposition is positive. *Considerable progress has been made in identifying and measuring social problems in our society.* Much more is known about who is poor or sick or badly educated, and this knowledge itself has helped clarify policy choices.

The second proposition is also positive. *Systematic analysis has improved our knowledge of the distribution of the initial costs and benefits of social action programs.* Much more is known about who wins and who loses.

The third proposition is negative. *Little progress has been made in comparing the benefits of different social action programs.* It is not possible, for example, to say whether it would do society more good to cure cancer or to teach poor children to read. I do not think this situation is temporary or that it matters much, for reasons explained in Chapter 3.

The fourth proposition, which is more important, is also negative. *Little is known about how to produce more effective health, education, and other social services.* Unfortunately, moreover, neither social service systems nor federal programs are organized to find out. Chapter 4 discusses this dismal state of affairs and the reasons for it.

If these propositions are correct, what can be done to improve the situation? Chapter 5 discusses the potentialities of social experimentation and makes the case for judicious use of this new technique to improve the effectiveness of social services.

But even if we knew how to produce more effective services, how would we insure that these methods were actually used? How can producers of social services be induced to do a more effective job? How can they be held accountable to the taxpayers and to the communities they serve? Chapter 6 discusses the concept of "accountability," what it might mean, and how it might work.

2 Who Wins and Who Loses?

The first step in making public policy is to get a picture of what the problem is. Social action programs should be based on answers to questions like these: How many people are poor? Who are they? Where are they? Why are they poor? Who is in bad health? Who is not receiving treatment? How many people need more education or better job skills? How are these social problems related to each other?

Statisticians and analysts have worked hard on these questions in the last few years. For their efforts they get high marks: *We know a lot more than we did about the distribution of social problems in our society.* We have much more detailed and usable knowledge about who is poor or sick or inadequately educated. This knowledge has exploded some myths and thrown a good deal of light on policy choices.

What Are the Problems?

The distribution of social problems has been illuminated by two important technical developments. The first is the improvement and wider use of sample survey techniques. The second is the astonishing increase in the data processing capacity of computers.

Surveys, of course, are not new. A census has been taken every decade since 1790 and social and economic characteristics of the population have been tabulated for some time. Until recently, however, census and other survey information was of limited usefulness to those interested in the interrelations of social characteristics. Data were usually displayed in tables in which only two or three characteristics could be considered at once. It was not possible to establish the simultaneous distribution of, or relation among, a large number of characteristics—say, age, race, sex, income, work experience, education, region, and number of children—either because the sample was too small or because the computation was too involved and expensive.

In late 1963, when the launching of the war on poverty was under consideration, those who made the decision had only the vaguest notions about how many people were poor and who they were. The Council of Economic Advisers picked $3,000 as the "poverty line" for family income even though everyone, including the council, was dissatisfied with the criterion.[1] Quite apart from the question of its level, it did not allow for the facts that larger families need higher incomes, that it costs more to live in a city than on a farm, and that prices rise over time. At that time, however, a more sophisticated definition could not have been used even if it had been available. No technical capability existed for estimating quickly from the census, or any other source, the characteristics of the poor according to more complex definitions.

Now, less than eight years later, the situation has entirely changed. More sensitive and useful definitions of poverty, which take into account family size, place of residence, and other characteristics, have been developed. A special census survey, the Survey of Economic Opportunity (SEO), has been designed to yield more detailed and more accurate information about low-income groups. From this and other surveys, masses of information have been collected, detailing the characteristics and whereabouts of the poor. One can now literally punch a button and find out how many of the poor, by any appropriate definition, are black or aged or have six children or work full-time or live in cities. This does not solve the problem of poverty,

1. *Economic Report of the President together with the Annual Report of the Council of Economic Advisers, January 1964*, p. 59. (This document is referred to hereafter as *Economic Report, 1964*.)

but it certainly helps in establishing what and where the problem is.

Making the survey data useful has involved ingenuity and hard work, because in raw form they leave much to be desired. Certain kinds of people—especially the poor and men in their twenties—tend to be missed or fail to respond to surveys. Certain kinds of questions are often answered inaccurately or not at all. On the average, people underreport their incomes. There is evidence, for example, of considerable underreporting of transfer income (social security benefits, welfare payments, and the like) on the Survey of Economic Opportunity.[2] Many manhours have gone into improving survey accuracy, estimating missing data, devising ways of merging different files of data on the same people, and otherwise improving the consistency and usefulness of survey information.[3]

Better statistics on poverty have influenced the way people think about the problem and have dispelled some myths and false impressions. For example, the first analyses of poverty based on the Council of Economic Advisers' $3,000 definition created the impression that a very high proportion of the poor are aged.[4] More refined criteria, such as that of the Social Security Administration, which allows variations by family size in the definition of poverty income, show the proportion of aged persons in the poor population to be considerably lower. It is lower still if an allowance is made for assets as well

2. Benjamin A. Okner, "Transfer Payments: Their Distribution and Role in Reducing Poverty" (paper prepared for delivery at the 134th meeting of the American Association for the Advancement of Science, December 1969; processed).

3. See, for example, Nelson McClung, John Moeller, and Eduardo Siguel, "Transfer Income Program Evaluation," Working Paper 950-3 (Urban Institute, Oct. 16, 1970; processed).

4. *Economic Report, 1964*, Chart 8, p. 63.

as income, since older persons are much more likely than the young to own their own homes or to have savings. While the plight of the aged poor should not be minimized, more refined definitions and statistics on poverty have rightly tended to dramatize the fact that a high proportion of the poor are children and relatively young heads of families.

The popular myth that most of the poor are black mothers with lots of children living in big cities also disappears quickly when the numbers are examined. Although many of the poor are, indeed, black mothers with several children, most are white and over half of all poor families have male heads. This distribution appears even in analyses using the Social Security Administration definition of poverty (about $3,700 for a family of four), and the proportions of white families and of those with male heads rise as the poverty line is set higher.

Another myth that will not stand up to the statistics is that poverty is largely a problem of people who cannot or will not work. About 55 percent of all poor families in 1969 had members who worked full- or part-time and almost a third were headed by males who worked full-time.[5] Sheer numbers are persuasive. The statistics dramatized the plight of the working poor and focused attention on the inadequacy of an income-transfer system designed to aid only those who could not work.

Poverty is not the only social problem whose incidence is now more fully understood. In 1965, when the Elementary and Secondary Education Act was under consideration, those who formulated it had only general notions of the nature, extent, and distribution of educational disadvantage among children from low-income and minority families. Better measures and

5. U.S. Bureau of the Census, *Current Population Reports*, Series P-60, No. 76, "24 Million Americans—Poverty in the United States: 1969" (1970), p. 59.

more data were needed. The Coleman report[6] was the first attempt on a national scale to measure the performance of school children by race and socioeconomic group and to compare the conditions under which they were being educated.[7] Perhaps the Coleman report did not explode any myths about educational attainment. Most people suspected that, on the average, poor children and black children did not do well in school, but the report confirmed and documented their suspicions. It showed that poor children start school less well prepared than children from average-income families. The absolute gap in their performance widens as they move through school, although the relative gap stays about the same. Being black compounds the problem.

The statistics bolstered arguments that federal attention should be focused on improving the education of low-income children. The HEW program memorandum on education prepared in connection with the budget for fiscal year 1969 used the Coleman statistics in support of the department's decision to put more of its resources for education into programs for disadvantaged children.[8] The memorandum did not allege that these programs for poor children were effective. It simply pointed out the magnitude of their needs and suggested that more resources, if well used, might be expected to alleviate them.

6. James S. Coleman and others, *Equality of Educational Opportunity* (U.S. Department of Health, Education, and Welfare, 1966).

7. Project TALENT, the 1960 survey conducted by the University of Pittsburgh for the U.S. Office of Education, was a national sample, but it related to high school only, did not collect racial information, and was not well adapted to socioeconomic comparisons. John C. Flanagan and others, *Project TALENT: The American High-School Student* (University of Pittsburgh, 1964).

8. U.S. Department of Health, Education, and Welfare, "Program Memorandum on Education Programs of DHEW, Fiscal Years 1969–1973" (Nov. 1, 1967; processed).

Health offers another example of the use of better survey data. In 1966, responding to interest that President Johnson expressed, HEW undertook an analysis designed to lead to a program for improving child health. All who participated—physicians, economists, and statisticians—were amazed at how difficult it was to assemble hard facts about the health status of children. Even with the full statistical resources of the federal government to draw upon, it was astonishingly difficult to put together a picture of the prevalence of serious illness and handicapping conditions among children. The information had to be pieced together from various sources and confidence in its accuracy was low.[9]

But children were not the only group about whose health we were ignorant. It was very difficult, for example, to make any estimate of the potential need for vocational rehabilitation services, since information on the prevalence of handicapping conditions among adults was not available.

The gap in knowledge about health is not yet filled, but the U.S. National Health Survey, which involves periodic sampling of individuals about their health, with medical examinations for some, is a long step in the right direction.[10] Such surveys are gradually adding to our knowledge of the health status of the

9. U.S. Department of Health, Education, and Welfare, Office of the Assistant Secretary for Program Coordination, *Program Analysis: Maternal and Child Health Care Programs*, Program Analyses, 1966-2 (October 1966); and Joseph S. Wholey, "The Absence of Program Evaluation as an Obstacle to Effective Public Expenditure Policy: A Case Study of Child Health Care Programs," in *The Analysis and Evaluation of Public Expenditures: The PPB System*, A Compendium of Papers Submitted to the Subcommittee on Economy in Government of the Joint Economic Committee, 91 Cong. 1 sess. (1969), Vol. 1, pp. 451–71.

10. See U.S. Department of Health, Education, and Welfare, National Center for Health Statistics, *Origin, Program and Operation of the U.S. National Health Survey* (reprinted 1965).

nation and of the extent to which health problems are being met.

Although survey methods and computer technology have made possible much better understanding of the distribution of social problems and their interrelations, there are some obviously important questions on which almost no information has been collected. For example, how do working mothers arrange for the care of their children, and how many children get inadequate care?

Moreover, most surveys are one-shot cross-sections. They tell nothing about what happens to the same people over time. There is a pressing need for longitudinal information to help us understand, for example, what happens to children as they move through a school system. Are children who have serious deficiencies in first grade necessarily the ones who are deficient in high school? What happens to people with health problems? To what extent do people move in and out of poverty?

The technical capacity to answer these questions now exists. Individuals and families can be assigned identifying numbers, such as the social security number that most people already have, which can be used to match data from different sources or on the same persons at different times. The crucial questions now are not so much technical as organizational. Can the collection of information, especially information on individuals at different points in their lives, be organized to be useful to policy makers without undue inconvenience or danger to privacy?[11]

11. *The Computer and Invasion of Privacy*, Hearings before a Subcommittee of the House Committee on Government Operations, 89 Cong. 2 sess. (1966); *The Coordination and Integration of Government Statistical Programs*, Hearings before the Subcommittee on Economic Statistics of the Joint Economic Committee, 90 Cong. 1 sess. (1967).

Knowing what the problems are, of course, is just the beginning. The next question is what to do about them. Intelligent choice among public programs depends in part on knowing who would benefit from a policy and who would pay its costs. In recent years, analysts have worked hard on this range of questions, and with some success: *More is known about the initial benefits and costs of social action programs, especially where these benefits are monetary.* More is known about who wins and who loses.

This proposition can perhaps be illustrated best by two major policy problems in which analyses of the distribution of the costs and benefits have played major roles. The first is the problem of designing an effective income maintenance system. The second is the problem of financing higher education.

Income Maintenance

The policy debate over income maintenance and welfare reform that preceded the development of President Nixon's family assistance plan provides a wealth of illustrations both of the usefulness and of the limitations of statistical analysis in the formulation of public policy. What follows is not a definitive history of this complex and still unfinished episode. It is, rather, an attempt to explain how policy makers, especially those in HEW, approached the problem, and to show where the contributions of statistical analysis were useful and where they were not.

The Welfare Problem

By the mid-1960s, concern about income maintenance programs was already high. Instead of a true income maintenance system, the United States had a patchwork of different programs, most of which had been designed in the 1930s to protect certain groups of individuals against certain types of income loss. The social security system was designed to insure contributors against income loss due to retirement, disability, and death of the breadwinner. Unemployment compensation was designed to protect covered workers from loss of income due to unemployment. Public assistance programs were a last line of defense, designed to protect certain categories of people who could not work and were not adequately covered by social insurance. Federal aid was provided for state programs of public assistance to the aged, the blind, and the permanently and totally disabled, and to certain families with dependent children.

It was clear that this patchwork system was not solving the problem of poverty in the 1960s. Despite general prosperity and rising levels of employment, millions were still poor—about 29.7 million by 1966, by the Social Security Administration's definition of poverty.[12] The poor fared unevenly under existing income maintenance programs, depending on where they lived and why they were poor. In general, public assistance benefits were more nearly adequate for the aged, the blind, and the disabled than for families with children, but benefit levels under all programs varied widely by state.

Of the whole complex of income maintenance programs, aid to families with dependent children (AFDC), primarily a program for families with no male breadwinner, was the most criticized for unfairness and inadequacy. Benefit levels varied widely and were unconscionably low in the poor states of the South. Moreover, millions of poor children were not covered at all. Federal law permitted states to extend benefits to families with an unemployed father, but fewer than half the states did so. No federal assistance was available if the father was em-

12. Mollie Orshansky, "The Shape of Poverty in 1966," *Social Security Bulletin*, Vol. 31 (March 1968), p. 5.

ployed. The vast majority of poor families with a male head were not covered at all. In 1966, 4½ million children lived in families with a male head who was working full- or part-time but not earning enough to keep the family out of poverty.[13]

The exclusion of families with male heads not only seemed unfair, but created some perverse incentives. Low-income men could improve the lot of their families by leaving them, thus making them eligible for welfare, and mothers already on welfare were discouraged from marrying lest they lose their welfare benefits. It was clear that these monetary incentives existed. It was not clear how many families actually responded to them. The number of broken families was rising but there was no evidence to show how much, if any, of the rise was due to the perverse incentives built into the welfare system.

Similarly, differences in the levels of benefits created incentives for families to move from poorer to richer states. Again, it was not clear what part, if any, of the substantial migration from the South to northern industrial areas was a response to welfare differentials.

The multiplicity of categories and interstate differentials made the welfare system extraordinarily complex and led to the imposition of stringent and potentially abusive administrative regulations. In an effort to prevent families from migrating in search of higher benefits, states imposed residence requirements and eligibility rules that were often arbitrary. Efforts to keep out the ineligible poor, especially families that included males of working age, led to the man-in-the-house rule and other demeaning attempts to police the lives of welfare mothers.[14]

13. *Ibid.*, p. 17.

14. Seventeen states had rules to cut off AFDC payments if the local welfare department found any evidence of the presence of a man. The contention was that he should be held financially responsible for the children's support. In April

Public assistance was not only complex, demeaning, inequitable, and inadequate; it was also becoming more and more expensive and burdensome to the states. Despite prosperity and high employment, welfare rolls were rising rapidly in the mid-1960s—no one was sure exactly why. Most of the increase was occurring in a few big industrial states—New York, California, Illinois, and Ohio. The explanation apparently lay in a combination of factors: liberalized standards of eligibility, increasing numbers of broken families, migration from the South to the North and West, and an increase in the proportion of eligible families applying for benefits. But these explanations were based on fragmentary statistics. Although periodic surveys revealed some characteristics of the total welfare population, there were no data that would indicate what *new* welfare families were like, where they came from, or how they differed from families already on the rolls.[15]

Diversity of Solutions

In the last three years of the Johnson administration a heated debate arose over income maintenance and welfare reform.

1970, the Supreme Court reaffirmed a 1968 ruling that states may not cut off AFDC payments unless the man actually contributes to the support of the children. *Congressional Quarterly Weekly Report*, Vol. 28 (April 24, 1970), p. 1134.

15. This data problem has not yet been solved. In 1968, a task force under the chairmanship of James F. Kelly recommended drastic changes in data collection on public assistance and medicaid; see *Report of the State-Federal Task Force on Costs of Medical Assistance and Public Assistance* (U.S. Department of Health, Education, and Welfare, 1968). The task force recommended that all states obtain information on the characteristics of recipients by frequent sampling from two populations: (1) those registered for or receiving public assistance; (2) cases opened, closed, or otherwise acted upon. Data not available on case records would be obtained by interview or questionnaire. Implementation of these recommendations would greatly improve estimates of how the public assistance caseload was changing and why, but so far, progress has been slow.

Fairly wide agreement had been reached on what was wrong with the existing welfare system. There was also considerable agreement on general objectives to be sought in improving income maintenance: to raise the incomes of the poor; to narrow disparities among states in benefit levels; to reduce inequities in the treatment of different kinds of poor people; to increase incentives to work; to remove incentives to break up families. There were, however, differing views on how to achieve these objectives. At least three major approaches had their spokesmen both within and outside the administration.

One approach was that of the "welfare reformers," who believed that the existing welfare system should be improved by a series of amendments to make it more uniform and more nearly adequate. The agenda for reform typically included federal action to put a floor under benefit levels, which would raise benefits in the South and tend to reduce the interstate disparities. Welfare reformers generally favored an increase in the federal contribution to welfare costs to reduce the burden on state taxpayers and to make it feasible for the poorer states to meet the federal minimum, and some favored eventual federal assumption of the full costs of welfare. Federal intervention was advocated to insure more humane and less punitive administration of welfare: elimination of the man-in-the-house rule, substitution of an income affidavit for the complex and demeaning means test to establish eligibility for welfare, and reduction of state residence requirements. Some advocated full federal administration of welfare programs.

The welfare reform position was strongly stated in an advisory panel report to the Secretary of HEW in 1966.[16] Within the administration, Wilbur Cohen was an articulate and effective advocate, who worked for a variety of measures to increase

16. Advisory Council on Public Welfare, "*Having the Power, We Have the Duty*," Report to the Secretary of Health, Education, and Welfare (HEW, 1966).

federal funding, widen coverage, and improve administration of the system. By 1968, he was advocating a fully federalized national welfare system.

A different basic approach was put forth by the advocates of a negative income tax. This group believed that reforming welfare was hopeless. To them the words "welfare" and "public assistance" implied punitive rules, meddling social workers, degradation and humiliation of the poor. They believed that the welfare apparatus should be scrapped in favor of a universal system of income transfers based on need and entirely separate from any other kind of social services. The new system would guarantee everyone a minimum income and would encourage recipients to work because only a moderate proportion of their earnings would be deducted from the minimum guarantee. For example, the guarantee might be set at $3,000 for a family of four and the proportion of earnings deducted (the marginal tax rate) at 50 percent. Under such a system a family with no earnings would receive $3,000, one with $2,000 would receive $2,000 for a total income of $4,000, and a family earning $6,000, the break-even point, would receive no government benefit.

This proposal seemed to some a logical extension of the principle of the progesssive income tax. Indeed, it was suggested that the most dignified system to administer it would be the income tax mechanism. Everyone would file a declaration of his income; most would pay taxes as they do now, but those at the low end of the income scale would receive payments (negative taxes) just as those who overpay their tax receive refunds. Hence, this type of proposal became known as a negative income tax, although its administration by the Internal Revenue Service was not an integral part of it.

The negative income tax had great appeal for academic economists, although most politicians and laymen found it a far-out, "egghead" idea. In the mid-1960s, as economists elaborated the theory and embodied it in practical proposals,[17] strong support developed in the Office of Economic Opportunity. Joseph Kershaw, the first planning officer of OEO, advocated the negative income tax as a major weapon of the war on poverty as early as 1965, and much work on the proposals was done under Kershaw and his successor, Robert Levine.[18]

The third major approach to income maintenance under active discussion was the family or children's allowance. Advocates of the allowance also believed that the welfare system should be dismantled, but they rejected the negative income tax, principally because it involved an income test. They believed that if people had to prove they were needy to get help, a stigma would always be attached to the help and that the simplest and most dignified way to insure a minimum income for needy children would be to give an allowance to *all* children regardless of need. Since a high proportion of poor families include children, such an allowance would contribute much to raising the incomes of the poor.[19]

The children's allowance had strong advocates both in and out of government. Perhaps its most articulate spokesman

17. See Christopher Green, *Negative Taxes and the Poverty Problem* (Brookings Institution, 1967), for a comprehensive discussion of the issues; see also Milton Friedman, *Capitalism and Freedom* (University of Chicago Press, 1962), pp. 190–95; James Tobin, Joseph A. Pechman, and Peter M. Mieszkowski, "Is a Negative Income Tax Practical?" *Yale Law Journal*, Vol. 77 (November 1967), pp. 1–27 (Brookings Reprint 142); Robert J. Lampman, "Approaches to the Reduction of Poverty," in American Economic Association, *Papers and Proceedings of the Seventy-seventh Annual Meeting, 1964* (*American Economic Review*, Vol. 55, May 1965), pp. 521–29. The Friedman, Lampman, and Tobin plans are discussed in George H. Hildebrand, "Poverty, Income Maintenance, and the Negative Income Tax," Cornell University, New York State School of Industrial and Labor Relations, ILR Paperback No. 1 (Cornell University, 1967).

18. Robert A. Levine, *The Poor Ye Need Not Have With You: Lessons from the War on Poverty* (M.I.T. Press, 1970), p. 60.

19. A similar approach (sometimes called a demogrant or universal pension) could be taken to adult poverty, but most of the discussion in the 1960s centered on children.

within the administration—first at OEO and later at HEW—was Alvin Schorr.[20]

To some extent, the differences in these positions reflected conflicts of basic values that could not be resolved by analysis. Advocates of a children's allowance, for example, believe that an income test is inherently wrong and that society has a moral duty to insure every child the essentials of life without subjecting him or his parents to the humiliation of proving need. But the debate also involved differing views of what was politically feasible. Welfare reformers, for example, believed it was more realistic to build on what existed than to expect Congress to repeal existing statutes and substitute something as unfamiliar as a negative income tax. Others felt there was little hope of enacting a children's allowance because it appears to the public an inducement to the poor to have more children.

Still another point of difference was the amount of resources that should or could be devoted to income maintenance. Indeed, budget constraints probably influenced the policy choices in this period more than any other factor.

Policy Decisions and Budget Constraints

In the mid-1960s the federal budget for social action programs increased rapidly. Major new programs were enacted: the Higher Education Act of 1965; the Elementary and Secondary Education Act of 1965; medicare and medicaid; and the war on poverty as provided for in the Economic Opportunity Act. From fiscal year 1960 to fiscal year 1967, the HEW budget nearly tripled and OEO grew from nothing to an agency with a budget of $1.5 billion a year.[21]

By 1967, however, heavy military spending for the escalating

20. Alvin Schorr, *Poor Kids: A Report on Children in Poverty* (Basic Books, 1966).
21. *The Budget of the United States Government for the Fiscal Year ending June 30, 1968*, p. 198.

war in Vietnam and accelerating inflation had completely altered the outlook for additional domestic programs. Strenuous efforts were made to hold down domestic spending. Total HEW spending was still increasing only because of the "built-in" growth in existing programs, especially public assistance, medicare, and medicaid. Some programs, including college and hospital construction, were cut back, and virtually nothing was left for new initiatives.[22] Moreover, budget projections gave little reason to hope that substantial sums would be available for new social action programs in the future even if the war in Vietnam subsided. Unless taxes were raised, built-in increases in domestic programs and postponed military expenditures seemed likely to eat up much of the increase in the federal budget for several years to come.

The budget stringency had a profound influence on the income maintenance debate within the government, essentially ruling out serious consideration of the children's allowance. Since a children's allowance goes to all families with children, regardless of their need, and since most American families are not poor, it is an extremely inefficient way of getting money to the poor. A children's allowance of $50 per month per child would cost about $28 billion, but would not succeed in eliminating poverty.[23] With every prospect of continued budgetary stringency at the federal level, it did not seem sensible to "waste" a large fraction of the added income maintenance dollar on the nonpoor.

22. Charles L. Schultze, *Setting National Priorities: The 1971 Budget* (Brookings Institution, 1970), pp. 56, 59–60, 63.

23. *Poverty Amid Plenty; The American Paradox*, the Report of the President's Commission on Income Maintenance Programs (November 1969), p. 147. The $28 billion estimate assumes that the tax exemption for children is eliminated and the children's allowance is taxable. The gross cost (without these tax change offsets) would be about $41 billion.

The budget prospect also ruled out a negative income tax with a guarantee at or even near the poverty line. Such a plan (with a 50 percent tax rate) would cost well over $20 billion and would also entail substantial transfers to the nonpoor.[24]

Realism about the federal budget forced a redefinition of the policy problem. The question was no longer what kind of income maintenance system would be best. Rather, it was what could be done on a realistic budget to assist those most in need and reduce disparities among states and among different kinds of poor people. A "realistic budget" was not precisely defined, but $4 billion to $6 billion in additional federal funds seemed the most that could be hoped for in the first full year of a new program.

This way of structuring the problem led analysts in several parts of the government to the same conclusion: The best first step was the introduction of a negative income tax with a guarantee at a fairly low level (say, half to two-thirds of the poverty line). Such a plan would be efficient, in the sense that the additional money would go to the poor. It would give priority to raising the incomes of two groups: (1) families already eligible for welfare in states with benefit levels well below the poverty line; (2) families with male heads (the "working poor"), most of whom were not eligible for aid under either state or federal programs. By putting a floor under incomes and extending aid to the working poor, this plan would reduce the disparities in the existing welfare system and lay the foundation for its eventual replacement by a new general income maintenance system similar to the negative income tax.

The major disadvantage of this strategy, however, was that a negative income tax with a guarantee substantially below the

24. Green, *Negative Taxes and the Poverty Problem*, Plan D-1, Table 9-1, pp. 139, 141.

poverty line would make some poor families worse off than they were under the existing welfare system. In states whose welfare benefits for eligible families were already at or near the poverty line, some kind of supplementary public assistance would have to continue. That meant two systems, rather than one, but there seemed to be no way out of this dilemma within the budget constraint.

By early 1968 the planning and evaluation staff of HEW had coalesced around this approach and proposed a guarantee of $2,136 (for a family of four with no other income) and a 50 percent marginal tax rate.[25] It was then estimated that this program would require additional federal outlays by 1974 of $9 billion, of which $3 billion would be savings to the states. (These estimates now appear too high.) The plan was the first such proposal to receive serious consideration in HEW, although similar ideas had been developed in OEO.[26]

The planning and evaluation staff worked intensively on this approach during 1968, when it still seemed possible that President Johnson would make welfare reform proposals before he left office. We did not, however, have the full blessing of the Secretary of HEW, Wilbur J. Cohen. Cohen was already committed to his bold proposal for federalizing the existing welfare system. He believed coverage should be extended to the

25. This proposal, developed by Worth Bateman, then Deputy Assistant Secretary for Program Analysis (Income Maintenance and Social Service Programs), is described as "Alternative IV" in U.S. Department of Health, Education, and Welfare, Office of the Assistant Secretary (Planning and Evaluation), *Program Memorandum on Income Maintenance and Social and Rehabilitation Services Programs of DHEW, Fiscal Years 1970–1974* (November 1968), pp. III-6-20.

26. OEO's program planning documents were not made available to HEW. A public version of one OEO plan appeared, however, in Walter Williams and James M. Lyday, "The Case for a Negative Income Tax," *American Child*, Vol. 48 (Summer 1966), pp. 16–19. See also Walter Williams and James M. Lyday, "Income Sufficiency and the Aged Poor," *Quarterly Review of Economics and Business*, Vol. 8 (Spring 1968), pp. 19–25.

working poor in the long run but he did not believe such an extension was politically feasible in the short run. Cohen thought Congress would be far more receptive to such improvements as a federal floor under benefits.[27]

In any case, President Johnson was less interested in welfare reform than in education and health programs. Moreover, big legislative decisions are rarely made at the end of an administration. It would take a new team to tackle welfare reform.

The Family Assistance Plan

The new Republican administration came in with the conviction that "something had to be done about welfare," but without a clear commitment to a particular course of action. Like the previous administration, the new team encompassed a broad spectrum of views. Conservatives believed welfare spending should be cut and work requirements made more stringent. Liberals, who believed the system should be reformed to reduce inequities, realized that this would require more money. During the transition, Richard Nathan, now Assistant Director of the Office of Management and Budget, headed a task force that advocated increasing the federal contribution to welfare and raising benefits for existing categories of recipients in the states where they were lowest. Daniel P. Moynihan was known as an advocate of a children's allowance.[28]

27. If the family assistance plan passes, this normally astute political forecaster will have been proved wrong—for once—about the Congress. Cohen was perhaps right in one sense, however. It would have been politically impossible for a Democratic administration to have proposed extension of welfare to the working poor. Labor union opposition might have killed the proposal at the White House level, if not below.

28. See "The Case for a Family Allowance," adapted from testimony of Daniel P. Moynihan before a Subcommittee of the Senate Government Operations Committee, on the federal role in urban problems, in *New York Times Magazine*, Feb. 5, 1967, pp. 13, 68–73.

The new team went through many of the arguments that had occupied its predecessors, but their resolution came more quickly, in part because the basic analysis was already available. Since the budgetary constraint was still regarded as severe, children's allowances were again ruled out of consideration.

The consensus was that priority should be given to reducing inequities in the system that give rise to perverse incentives. A federal floor under welfare payments would reduce disparities between richer and poorer states. Covering the working poor would reduce disparities between families with male and female heads and would weaken incentives to break up families. To this end, a proposal was advanced for a new federal program of the negative tax type, with wide coverage, a low guarantee, and a moderate tax rate. Despite the difficulties in meshing this new system with the old one and maintaining a second supplementary system in states whose welfare payments were already above the new minimums, this approach appeared to be the best buy for the money.

Once the basic decision was made, the analysts were called on to estimate the costs of a large number of specific variations, and to determine what types of families would benefit from each, and how individual states would be affected. Three aspects of the basic plan could be adjusted: the guarantee level, the marginal tax rate, and the coverage. If, for example, the guarantee level for a family of four were raised from $1,600 to $1,700, the states would bear less burden for existing programs, and more people would be covered, but the program would be more expensive for the federal government. Lowering the tax rate by increasing the percentage of earnings a family was allowed to keep from 50 percent to, say, 60 percent, would promote incentives to work and raise total benefits, but would at the same time increase the cost of the program. Whether the basic program covered all individuals, or only families, or only families with children, would also affect its cost.

It was by no means obvious how much these variations would cost, what kinds of people would gain or lose, or how various modifications would affect the burden on particular states. Fortunately, by the time decisions were being made in early 1969, the analysts had a new tool. The SEO had been put on computer tape and programs written that would yield quick, detailed answers to these questions. Dozens of runs were done with minor variations before one version of the plan was chosen to send to Congress in October 1969. Dozens more were done at the request of the Congress as both houses considered possible changes in the bill.

The plan chosen by the Nixon administration for submission to Congress, known as the family assistance plan, was basically a negative income tax with a $1,600 guarantee for a family of four and a 50 percent marginal tax rate. Two important decisions had been made after looking at the costs of minor variations. The first, made in the interest of saving money, was to extend coverage of the plan only to families with children. The existing welfare programs for the adult poor (the aged, blind, and disabled) would be retained and federal contributions increased. But no aid was extended to poor families or individuals who had no children or did not fall in any existing welfare category.

The other decision was to allow each family to keep the first $60 a month ($720 a year) of its earnings without any reduction in its family assistance benefits. This "set-aside" was intended to increase incentives to work, although no one knew whether it would actually be effective. The set-aside was expensive, adding at least a half-billion dollars to the cost of the plan.

The necessity of meshing this apparently simple plan into

existing welfare programs created difficult dilemmas. An effort was made to ensure that no one covered by current programs would be worse off under the new system and that no state would have to put up additional funds. The existing system had grown so complicated, however, that achieving these ends within the budget constraint proved tricky, if not impossible. For example, some states had an official "standard of need" for existing welfare programs that was substantially higher than the actual payments, and families were allowed to keep all of their earnings up to this figure. Subjecting these families to the marginal tax rates of the new plan would make some of them worse off than they were before.

Another dilemma involved the policy of making payments to families with unemployed fathers. Where this program existed, benefits were the same as those for the regular AFDC program, and unemployed fathers were defined as those who worked fewer than thirty-five hours a week. In states that had benefits above family assistance levels, an odd situation arose. All low-income families would be covered even if the fathers worked full time, but their benefits would be lower. If the program for unemployed fathers were retained, the families eligible for it would be better off than families whose fathers worked full time for the same wages. Heads of the latter families thus had an incentive to reduce their hours of work to fewer than 35, perhaps by connivance with their employers. On the other hand, if the program for unemployed fathers were abolished, some families would suffer a cut in income. This dilemma could be resolved only by spending the money necessary to bring benefits for all working families up to the levels of the program for unemployed fathers.

Another tough problem brought to light, although not created, by the family assistance plan was the difficulty of maintaining work incentives when several different programs set benefits in relation to income. Under the family assistance plan the marginal tax rate was 50 percent—a family was allowed to keep half its earnings above the first $720 a year. If the family received supplementary state benefits, however, it was subject to a 66⅔ percent tax rate; its benefits would be reduced by two dollars for every three dollars it earned. These marginal rates were extremely high compared with rates facing middle-income families, but they were only the beginning. Benefits the family might receive under other income-tested programs—food stamps or medicaid or public housing—would fall as their earnings rose. Moreover, their earnings would be reduced by social security contributions and perhaps by regular income tax, so that the effective marginal tax rate on earnings might be 90 or 100 percent or even more. An increase in a family's earnings might even worsen its situation. This dilemma also had no solution except the provision of more money. Any attempt to reduce these marginal rates—singly or together—meant higher costs for the program affected.

The Role of Analysis

It is too soon to predict how this historical episode will end, although substantial welfare reform along the lines proposed by President Nixon now seems likely. In this development, analytical work played two important roles. First, as they pored over the numbers, policy makers as well as analysts gained new insights into what was wrong with the existing welfare system and arrived at new solutions to propose. For example, quite simple computations of the extent to which families in some states could increase their income by breaking into separate units served to focus attention on this perverse aspect of the welfare system.

Second, the analysts were asked at all stages to estimate the distribution of costs and benefits—who would win and who would lose—under alternative plans, and to compare them in terms of cost, effectiveness in reducing poverty, effect on incentives, and other factors, so that informed choices could be made.

From the beginning the analysts saw that their tools for answering these questions were woefully inadequate. What was needed was a behavioral model of the population—at least of the low-income population—that would make it possible to simulate the effects of alternative policies. *Step One* toward this goal would be to reproduce on a computer tape the characteristics of a sample of low-income families (size, sex of head, employment status, income by source, and other relevant characteristics), which could be used to try out different structures and levels of income maintenance. Estimates could be made of who would benefit and how much each alternative would cost—assuming that no changes in family composition or working behavior took place as a result of changes in income maintenance benefits. *Step Two* would be to draw on research and experimentation for estimates of these behavioral responses and to build these into the calculations. If, for example, one knew the effect of a higher level of income transfers on family formation or labor force participation, one could make better estimates of the impact of policy changes. *Step Three* would be to incorporate in the model the estimated effects on earnings of investments in people, such as education and training and health programs. It would then be possible to look not only at alternative income maintenance programs, but also at the trade-offs between income maintenance and alternative investment strategies against poverty.

As late as 1966, HEW analysts could not take even Step One.

A study done in that year, which attempted to analyze the effectiveness of present and prospective income maintenance programs in reducing poverty, could compile estimates of the income levels and other characteristics of individual programs, but it was hard to piece them together.[29] The report admitted that "existing data on sources of income of the poor are too sketchy for complete assessment of the contribution of existing programs to alleviation of poverty."[30] Fragmentary information was used, however, to show the effectiveness of social security and public assistance in reducing poverty and to indicate the magnitude of the remaining gaps. Alternative future policies, such as social security benefit increases, categorical and noncategorical welfare reforms, and two varieties of negative income tax, were specified, and rough estimates were made of their costs and effectiveness in narrowing the gap. But the estimation process was laborious and involved a good deal of guesswork, and it proved impossible to look at many alternatives. It was simply too much work.

Between 1966 and 1969, when the family assistance plan went to Congress, the analysts worked hard to develop Step One capability. A major input was the SEO, which contained some data not previously available and was designed specifically to yield a more reliable picture of the poverty population than previous surveys had done. There were many errors and omissions, however, and much effort went into cleaning up the data and improving the estimates by matching them with data from other sources.

The survey data, modified in various ways, proved a highly

29. U.S. Department of Health, Education, and Welfare, Office of the Assistant Secretary for Program Coordination, *Income and Benefit Programs*, Program Analysis 1966-6 (October 1966).

30. *Ibid.*, p. 13.

useful and flexible tool for estimating the costs of alternative versions of the family assistance plan and the distribution of benefits. The President's Commission on Income Maintenance Programs (called the Heineman Commission) also used these tapes in developing its proposal and the costs of alternatives. Moreover, their usefulness has not been confined to the federal establishment. They were used, for example, to make an estimate for George Wiley, of the National Welfare Rights Organization, of the cost and implications of a plan guaranteeing a $5,500 annual income to a family of four.

This simple estimating technique has greatly aided the intelligent consideration of alternative income maintenance proposals. It has replaced back-of-the-envelope guesswork and allowed the discussants to focus on the real issues rather than wrangling over how to get cost estimates. But it is still just Step One.

Apart from the inaccuracies and biases that time will reveal, the survey data are limited in that they make no allowance for changes in behavior that might result from changes in income maintenance programs. For a modest income maintenance proposal like the family assistance plan, the assumption that people will go on working at the same rate and living in the same groups they do now is probably not far wrong. However, a significantly different program might be expected to alter patterns of living and working, perhaps drastically. While some arbitrary assumptions could be made about changes in labor force behavior and family groupings, almost nothing is known about how such behavior would respond to various income maintenance policies. How many people would quit work if they were guaranteed $3,000 a year? How many young people or old people would maintain their own households if they could afford to do so? How many more marriages would take place if economic incentives were different? Experiments of the type discussed in Chapter 5 may hold the key to such questions and provide a basis for Step Two: a true model of the behavior of the population in response to changes in income maintenance programs. Systematic experimentation with training, education, and human investment programs will also be necessary before we can take Step Three: a behavioral model of the population from which it will be possible to estimate the relative effectiveness of income maintenance and investment strategies.

The "Tax Model"

Advances in computer technology have improved estimates of who "wins," that is, who benefits from income transfers, and who "loses"—who is affected by changes in tax rates and tax structures. In particular, our understanding of who bears the burden of changes in the federal income tax has been enhanced by the introduction of the so-called "tax model." This new tool is simply a sample of federal tax returns entered on computer tape, along with programs to give estimates of the increase or decrease in tax yield, and of the distribution of effects among various taxpayers, that would accompany various changes in the base or rate structure of the federal income tax.[31]

The tax model has the same limitations as the SEO: It does

31. For a description of the tax return file, see Joseph A. Pechman, "A New Tax Model for Revenue Estimating," in Alan T. Peacock and Gerald Hauser (eds.), *Government Finance and Economic Development* (Paris: Organisation for Economic Co-operation and Development, 1965), pp. 231–44 (Brookings Reprint 102); and "The Brookings 1966 Federal Individual Income Tax File," Brookings Computer Center Memorandum No. 42 (June 30, 1968; processed). For an example of the use of this tool, see Joseph A. Pechman and Benjamin A. Okner, "Simulation of the Carter Commission Tax Proposals for the United States," *National Tax Journal*, Vol. 22 (March 1969), pp. 2–23 (Brookings Reprint 159).

not reflect changes in behavior of individuals and families that might occur as a consequence of tax changes. It is a highly useful tool for analyzing the distributional effects of tax changes when it can reasonably be assumed that the behavioral effects will be relatively small.

Higher Education

In the late 1960s much concern was exhibited in Washington about the financial "crisis" in higher education and what the federal government should do about it. Although the importance of doing something was not as obvious in higher education as it was in welfare, nevertheless many believed that the system soon would break down or seriously deteriorate if the federal government did not take a hand.

There were at least three views of the problem.[32] First, and most vocally expressed, was the view of the colleges and universities, which, faced with rapidly rising costs due to expanding enrollment, rising salaries, and greater building and other costs, could find no new cost-saving techniques for imparting information to young minds. Only a few institutions—mostly small and private—were in immediate financial danger; but most were apprehensive about their financial future. Private institutions, largely dependent on tuition, worried that they would lose students if they continued to raise prices. Public institutions, heavily dependent on tax support, were concerned that legislatures would stop voting increases in funds and tighten up on higher education budgets. Both public and private institutions were frustrated by the complexity of special-purpose federal programs and were seeking a more stable source of funds. They believed that, without a change in financing arrangements, the

32. For a discussion of different viewpoints and policies, see Ronald A. Wolk, *Alternative Methods of Federal Funding for Higher Education* (Carnegie Commission on the Future of Higher Education, 1968).

nation would not put enough resources into higher education. They were—not surprisingly—attracted to the idea of general federal support of institutions of higher education.

Students and their families confronted rising tuition and college living costs that made it hard to meet educational expenses, especially where there was more than one child in college or a preference for private education. Even those with good incomes complained that the present system put too much of the financial burden on students and their families. They pressured Congress to keep the price down by aiding institutions, to make loans and grants available to students, or to give parents of college students a tax break. Proposals for income tax credits several times came close to enactment.

A third view, less vocally expressed in Washington, was that of the nonstudents—those who were in large part excluded from higher education. Although enrollments had risen rapidly in the 1950s and 1960s, higher education was still primarily a privilege of middle- and upper-income groups. Young people from low-income families—especially if they were also black, Indian, or Spanish-speaking—had little chance of getting a college education. To these groups, the crisis was clearly one of equalizing opportunities. They favored providing access to free public education for everyone, or greatly increasing student aid funds, or both.

The higher education problem resembled the income maintenance problem in one sense: The federal government had no coherent strategy to deal with it. A series of programs had accumulated to build college facilities and college housing; to provide scholarships, loans, fellowships, and traineeships to students; and to support research, especially in fields that seemed to have special national importance. But there was no general policy of supporting higher education, just as there was no general policy to assure the poor an adequate income.

As in income maintenance, extremely diverse positions developed on what ought to be done, some of them reflecting basically different points of view about the value of higher education or the role of government in financing it. Some saw no need for special federal action, or thought it should be confined to traditional areas of federal concern, like support of science. Those who advocated new federal action fell into two groups. Advocates of institutional aid believed that colleges and universities were the best judges of how to spend higher education funds wisely. Advocates of student aid believed that putting purchasing power in the hands of students would tend to make institutions more responsive to student needs, although some favored increased loans, others favored increased grants, and still others conceded room for both.

Higher education had attracted the attention of economists in the 1950s and 1960s. Most of their analyses were concerned with the distribution of higher education benefits and costs. What did the analysts have to contribute to this complex policy question?

Higher education clearly benefits those who receive it—on the average. People who attend colleges and universities tend to earn more than those who do not. Even without the additional education, they probably would have earned somewhat more because of higher average ability or motivation, but at least part of their superior earning power can be regarded as a return on the investment in their education. Economists in the 1960s put considerable effort into estimating such effects and computing rates of return on different types of education.[33] The results indicated that higher education is a moderately good

33. See, for example, W. Lee Hansen, "Total and Private Rates of Return to Investment in Schooling," *Journal of Political Economy*, Vol. 71 (February 1963), pp. 128–40; and Gary Becker, *Human Capital: A Theoretical and Empirical Analysis with Special Reference to Education* (Columbia University Press for the National Bureau of Economic Research, 1964).

investment for society as a whole; rates of return are in the same range as returns on physical capital investment. For the average student, however, higher education is an excellent investment since he pays only part of the cost of improving his future earning power. This result has led some to conclude that students should bear a larger part of the cost.

Not all the benefits of higher education, however, are reflected in individual incomes. Many students would seek higher education for the enjoyment and cultural enrichment it provides even if it did not enhance their earnings. Moreover, higher education benefits the entire community, not simply those who receive it, by promoting research and innovation and raising the cultural level of the society. These public benefits are hard to isolate and measure. Analysts have talked about them, but have done little to quantify them. If the public benefits are large, however, they would justify considerable public investment and perhaps less, rather than more, reliance on charges paid by the student.

Opportunities for higher education and the way in which public subsidies for higher education benefited different income groups also drew analytical attention. Several studies in the 1950s and early 1960s documented the fairly obvious fact that opportunity for higher education is closely related to income. Project TALENT showed that high school students who scored high on an ability test were much more likely to go to college if they came from upper-income families than if they came from lower-income families.[34] These studies revealed considerable

34. For example, students ranking in the top 20 percent by high school achievement, as measured by test scores, had a 95 percent chance of going to college within five years of high school graduation *if* they came from the top family-income quartile. If they came from the lowest quartile they had only a 50 percent chance. See U.S. Department of Health, Education, and Welfare, Office of the Assistant Secretary for Planning and Evaluation, *Toward A Long-Range Plan for Federal Financial Support for Higher Education*, A Report to the President (1969), Table 1, p. 5 (based on Project TALENT data).

"talent loss": Many low-income students of high ability do not get the benefit of higher education, and there are major differences in opportunities at all ability levels.

Statistics relating college attendance to income prompted economists to take a look at the distributional effects of public subsidies in higher education. Who gains from the considerable amounts of tax money that go into the support of higher education, and who loses?

To the surprise of no one who had given the matter thought, the studies revealed that students from upper-income families tend to go to more costly public colleges (universities rather than four- or two-year colleges), and to attend them longer, than do students from lower-income families. The taxpayer is spending more funds for the well-to-do student than for the less affluent student.

In the study of public higher education in California, Hansen and Weisbrod found that the average annual subsidy per student at the University of California was about $1,700, and that the average family income of its students was $12,000. By contrast, the average subsidy at junior colleges in California was $720 and the average student came from a family with an income of $8,800.[35] Using rough estimates of the state and local taxes paid by families at these income levels, Hansen and Weisbrod concluded that "the current method of financing public higher education [in California] leads to a sizeable redistribution of income from lower to higher income."[36] This conclusion does not necessarily follow, however, as Pechman has pointed out.[37] Within

35. W. Lee Hansen and Burton A. Weisbrod, *Benefits, Costs, and Finance of Public Higher Education* (Markham, 1969), p. 76.

36. *Ibid.*, p. 77.

37. Joseph A. Pechman, "The Distributional Effects of Public Higher Education in California," *Journal of Human Resources*, Vol. 5 (Summer 1970), pp. 361–70.

income classes there is redistribution from those who pay taxes (everybody) to those who benefit from the higher education (a much smaller proportion). To calculate the net redistribution from one income class to another requires estimation of the taxes paid by income classes for the support of higher education as well as the average use of the system and amount of the benefit. A rough attempt to make these estimates suggests that the greatest gainers from public higher education in California are actually middle-income groups. They are heavy users of the higher education system and, as a group, recoup more than their share of the taxes used to support it.[38] But, no matter how the taxes are raised, state funds for higher education apparently benefit institutions frequented by the middle class and the rich more heavily than those the poor attend.

David Mundel has recently attempted to show how various federal moneys to support higher education (including income tax benefits) are distributed among income classes.[39] Although some federal programs are skewed toward low-income students, others have the opposite effect. On balance, federal subsidies seem to be distributed by income class roughly the same as students are.

Edward Denison has looked at the distribution of subsidies from a somewhat different point of view.[40] He estimated the total subsidy to higher education (expenditures minus charges to students) by academic ability of students (high school grades). The calculations are rough, but their results are unmistakable: Higher education subsidies go heavily to those who by conven-

38. Robert W. Hartman, "A Comment on the Pechman-Hansen-Weisbrod Controversy," *Journal of Human Resources*, Vol. 5 (Fall 1970), pp. 519–23.

39. David S. Mundel, "Distribution of Federal Student Subsidies" (June 26, 1970; processed).

40. Edward F. Denison, "An Aspect of Inequality of Opportunity," *Journal of Political Economy*, Vol. 78 (September/October 1970), pp. 1195–1202.

tional academic standards are already well endowed. Those who do well in high school (especially if they are boys) receive many times the subsidy given to those who do not.

These simple computations serve largely to dramatize facts already known. No one really thought that higher education gave disproportionate subsidies to the poor or to the academically less qualified. But the dramatization has forced some thought about whether the present system distributes higher education subsidies in a desirable way. If the private benefits of higher education are substantial, should scarce public funds be used to distribute them to those who can afford to pay for them and to those who might be expected to make it on their own?

In his education message in February 1968, President Johnson asked the Secretary of HEW to "begin preparing a long-range plan for the support of higher education in America." This charge resulted in a report and a series of recommendations issued just before the end of the Johnson administration.[41] The study did not attempt to tackle the difficult question of measuring public and private benefits. It assumed that both kinds flowed from higher education, and that partial subsidization by several levels of government should continue. Rather, in response to the President's charge, the study made a serious effort to identify the objectives of *federal* support for higher education, and alternative ways of accomplishing them.

Of the six objectives listed, two figured most prominently in the study: (1) improving the equality of opportunity for higher education, and (2) improving its quality.[42]

It is not easy to define equality of opportunity for higher education, but it is not hard to show that on any reasonable definition we do not have it now. The study emphasized the

41. *Toward a Long-Range Plan.* Quote is from p. iii.

42. *Ibid.*, pp. 3–4.

differences in college enrollment rates among lower- and higher-income high school graduates of the same ability level, and also pointed out that young people from lower-income groups are less likely than those from upper-income families to finish high school or to score well on achievement tests.[43]

The quality of higher education is even harder to define, and the study simply assumed a positive correlation between quality of education and quantity of resources devoted to each student. An examination of trends in resources per student in various types of institutions revealed no evidence that quality in this sense was declining. Despite rapid increases in enrollment, institutions of higher education as a group had managed to expand their resources quite rapidly.

> For all institutions, revenues per student increased at an average annual rate of 5.5 percent during the period from 1959–60 to 1965–66.
>
> There was a marked disparity in the rates of increase in revenues per student in public and private institutions, with public institutions' revenues per student increasing 4.0 percent annually while the comparable rate of increase for private institutions was 8.1 percent.[44]

In other words, no evidence was found that private institutions as a group were suffering a decline in quality. On the contrary, private institutions—especially private universities—seemed to be offering education of increasingly higher quality to a declining fraction of the student population.

The study then examined the major available tools by which the federal government might increase equality of opportunity and resources per student. The conclusion—hardly a startling one—was that different tools are appropriate to different objec-

43. *Ibid.*, pp. 6–7.

44. *Ibid.*, p. 11. See also Alice M. Rivlin and June O'Neill, "Growth and Change in Higher Education," in Robert H. Connery (ed.), *The Corporation and the Campus: Corporate Support of Higher Education in the 1970s*, Proceedings of the Academy of Political Science, Vol. 30, No. 1 (The Academy, 1970), pp. 66–74.

tives. If priority were given to increasing equality of opportunity, then assistance to students based on need seemed likely to be most effective. Aid to institutions might serve to keep tuition down, but would help mainly those who could afford to go to college anyway. Like the children's allowance, a general institutional subsidy appeared to be an inefficient way to reach those in need, although it could be used to induce institutions to expand their enrollments and to take in high-risk students.

As a result of this study, HEW recommended that the federal government give priority to equalizing opportunity for higher education and budget a major increase in federal aid to students. Its recommendations included grants to needy students, sufficient to guarantee that all who could gain admission to a college or university could go; a federal loan bank to help students from all income levels; and cost-of-education allowances to be paid to colleges and universities that accepted students receiving federal aid.[45]

A report of the Carnegie Commission on Higher Education, issued at about the same time, also emphasized equality of opportunity for higher education.[46] It recommended a similar set of federal programs including student grants based on need, a loan bank, and cost-of-education allowances.

Of what help were the analysts? Surely one did not need much analysis to come to the conclusion that student aid would be a good way to get poor students into college! People had advocated student aid for years without benefit of systems analysis. The analysis served largely to clarify the dimensions of the problem, to identify more readily those who would benefit from

45. *Toward a Long-Range Plan*, pp. 31–35.

46. Carnegie Commission on Higher Education, *Quality and Equality: New Levels of Federal Responsibility for Higher Education* (McGraw-Hill, 1968). See also the Commission's *Quality and Equality: Revised Recommendations; New Levels of Federal Responsibility for Higher Education* (McGraw-Hill, 1970).

various kinds of programs, and to establish their approximate costs.

Like the income maintenance analyses, the higher education studies were weakened by an almost complete absence of behavioral information. Virtually no basis existed for estimating how students and institutions would react to changes in government programs. How many students would go to college, or drop out, if prices or student aid were altered? How many students would borrow under various terms and conditions of loans? These questions could be answered only by guesses.

Moreover, the study concentrated entirely on distributional questions—on how to improve access to higher education. It did not deal with the value to the nation of higher education compared with other claims on the public treasury. It did not suggest ways to produce higher education more effectively, nor did it treat alternative arrangements, like on-the-job training, that might accomplish some of the ends now served by higher education. Subsequent chapters turn to the problems of answering such questions.

3 What Does the Most Good?

The last chapter expressed a sanguine view of the progress made by analysts in the social action area. The advances in measuring the distribution of social problems or needs and in identifying who could win and who would lose from particular social action programs have led to better-informed decisions on welfare, higher education, and other social action programs.

The big difficulty, however, is that there are so many social problems. Action could be taken in so many fields—from preschool to graduate education, from training welders to feeding infants, from biochemical research to welfare payments. It is not possible to do everything at once. The problem facing decision makers is the classic economic problem of allocating scarce resources among competing ends. What would do the most good? What do the analysts have to say about the *comparative* value of social action programs?

To be useful in answering these questions, the analysts must do two things. The first step is to identify the objectives of education, health, and other social action programs and to develop measures of progress toward these objectives. The second step is to find a way of comparing the benefits to the nation of moving toward these various objectives.

Identifying the Objectives

Social action programs are sometimes described as "soft," in contrast with the "hard" programs like defense and space. The implication is that a major impediment to decision making in the social action area is lack of definable and measurable objectives.

Despite appearances, however, I believe there is a wide measure of agreement in the nation, if not about final goals, at least about desirable directions of change. The bitter argument that rages among the radical right, the middle, and the new and old left over social action programs is not primarily about the objectives themselves. The real issues are the relative importance of these and other objectives (curing poverty versus preserving self-reliance, for example) and the means of reaching them. Almost all the participants in the argument genuinely want healthier, better-educated citizens, and less poverty. These are not empty slogans. They suggest indicators—a set of measurements—that most people would accept at least with respect to the desirable direction of change. Most people believe infant mortality rates should go down, reading levels should go up, and the number of people with low incomes should decline. They are not agreed on what they would give up to achieve these changes, how to achieve them, or which ones are most important.

A number of social scientists have recently advocated the development of a comprehensive set of indicators to show social progress or retrogression, and the preparation of an annual "social report" that would attempt to assess the social health of the nation, much as the President's Economic Report assesses its economic health.[1] Toward the end of the last administration, the Department of Health, Education, and Welfare (HEW) explored the feasibility of social reporting and produced a document modestly (and appropriately) entitled, *Toward a Social Report.*[2] The exploration revealed monstrous gaps in available information. It did not, however, reveal much disagreement on

1. See, for example, Bertram M. Gross (ed.), *Social Goals and Indicators for American Society*, Vol. 1, *The Annals of The American Academy of Political and Social Science*, Vol. 371 (May 1967); and Eleanor B. Sheldon and Wilbert E. Moore (eds.), *Indicators of Social Change: Concepts and Measurements* (Russell Sage Foundation, 1968).

2. U.S. Department of Health, Education, and Welfare, *Toward a Social Report* (1969). The report was written under the direction of Mancur Olson.

what would be desirable indicators of progress or retrogression in health, education, and income status.

Almost everyone, for example, can accept, at least conceptually, a common set of measures that would indicate that the nation is getting healthier. Not all of these measures now exist and most of those that are available are negatively oriented. Infant mortality rates, death rates by age and by specific disease, days of bed disability, and indices of crippling and inability to function all measure some aspect of the ill health we are trying to reduce. One can, however, easily imagine a set of positive indicators of health, including physical measures of strength and vigor and attitudinal measures of healthy feelings. Modern survey techniques permit development of such a series, on whose desirable direction of movement most people could agree.

Education presents a more difficult case. One has to be especially careful not to take inputs for outputs: Much of the literature reads as though preventing dropouts and keeping children in school longer were ends in themselves. But even among educators there is a fairly wide measure of agreement on three types of objectives.

The first is improvement in basic intellectual skills—the ability to read, communicate, manipulate numbers, and handle scientific and mechanical concepts. Tests that are now available are, of course, far from perfect measures of how well people handle these skills. Many tests have cultural and linguistic biases that make them insensitive instruments for measuring the skills of minority groups, whose members may communicate skillfully in their own languages but fail tests given in standard English, loaded with middle-class words, and scored by middle-class values. It is surprising that more effort has not been devoted to constructing better tests. It is even more surprising that more effort has not been made to analyze the test data that are now collected. Schools do a great deal of testing and use the results, for better or worse, in the diagnosis and counseling of individual students, but rarely for analytical purposes—to compare the effectiveness of different programs or different schools, or to identify progress or retrogression of the system over time. Seeking an answer to the question, "Is the nation better educated than it used to be?" the authors of *Toward a Social Report* scoured the literature, and found almost nothing worth reporting. The much-disputed National Assessment of Education, a series of tests on various subjects to be administered periodically to a national sample of children and adults, promises at long last to provide some continuing information on the knowledge and basic intellectual skills of a cross-section of Americans.[3]

Besides basic intellectual skills, a second set of objectives in education might loosely be called the "ability to cope." Most people believe that an important objective of education is the development of self-confidence, a positive self-image, and the ability to deal with new situations. The schools have often failed here. The black power and black pride movements are in part a reaction to the dismal failure of schools to help black children feel pride and confidence in themselves. Measures of ability to cope are even more primitive and questionable than test scores, but in principle there seems to be no reason why they could not be developed.

The third set of objectives in education has to do with job

3. The assessment, which began in April 1969, while useful for showing changes at the national level, will be useless for showing how particular schools or school systems are performing. School officials, fearful that, for them, "assessment" meant "report cards," rejected all designs that would have permitted comparisons among schools or systems. See Martin T. Katzman and Ronald S. Rosen, "The Science and Politics of National Educational Assessment," *The Record*, Vol. 71 (May 1970), pp. 571–86.

skills and future income. There is general agreement that a good education prepares a student either for a good job or for the future education that will lead to one. Here again, surprisingly little effort has been made to measure the extent to which our schools, even our supposedly vocational schools, actually succeed in preparing students for jobs, but in principle their success or failure would not be impossible to measure.

The reduction of poverty also seems to be a generally accepted objective. Definitions of poverty differ, but most people would agree that they want, by some means, to raise the standard of living of the poorest Americans, and that this standard can be at least roughly measured in money income, corrected for price levels and family size. This does not mean that there is agreement on a desirable distribution of income, or on how much the rich should give up to help the poor; it means simply that raising the lowest end of the income distribution is generally thought to be desirable.

To be sure, in important areas of social concern objectives are vague and measures nonexistent. There is concern, for example, about the "alienation" of individuals from society, but little agreement on how to measure it or how much of it is just rugged individualism. Most people would like to see a reduction in individual criminal behavior, but many disagree on whether civil disorder is inherently bad. Are student riots a symptom of alienation and the breakdown of law and order, or are they evidence of social concern among the young and active who desire to make a better world?

Despite these gray areas, we seem to have fairly wide agreement on *some* objectives of social policy. We can at least conceive of ways to measure movement toward objectives for which we know the appropriate sign. The really difficult problems do not arise until we attempt to attach weights to these objectives so that we can allocate scarce resources among them —until we ask, "Which is more important, curing cancer or teaching poor children to read?"

Comparing the Benefits: Cancer Cure versus Reading

How can we compare the merits of a program to find a cure for cancer with those of a program to teach poor children to read? If resources are insufficient to do both, the orthodox answer of the economists is to add up the costs and benefits of each and choose the program with the higher excess of benefits over costs. Of course, it is unlikely to be an either-or decision. Resources can usually be allocated to both programs, and the question is how much to each. In this case, the task is to find out whether additional funds would bring more benefits in one program than in the other.

How helpful is cost-benefit analysis in the real world of social action decisions?

Our ability to estimate the costs of such programs is admittedly weak. The costs of finding a cure for cancer are inherently uncertain; they depend on unforeseeable outcomes of basic and applied research. At best, one could make an informed guess about the probability of success at various levels of funding. Teaching poor children to read, however, seems more amenable to cost estimation. In principle, one could examine successful reading programs, determine which ones showed most success per dollar expended, and estimate the costs of extending them to larger numbers of children. In fact, however, this has not been done. The problem of estimating the costs of alternative types of social action has not received nearly the attention that has been devoted to similar problems involving weapons systems. We will come back to the cost side in later chapters.

Unlike cost analysis, benefit measurement in the social action area has attracted some very good minds. Two conferences sponsored by the Brookings Institution, for example, have been devoted primarily to this subject, and the journal literature is substantial.[4]

In setting values on the benefits of public programs, the economist's first line of attack is market price: How does the market value *X* relative to *Y*? But market prices offer almost no help in valuing the outputs of social action programs, since they are not usually sold and thus have no price. If they are sold, it is under conditions of monopoly and great consumer ignorance, so their prices have little meaning. A cure for cancer is not sold because it does not exist. There is no widespread private market for reading instruction.

In the absence of market prices the economist turns to a second probing point: He attempts to estimate what people might be willing, or ought to be willing, to pay for the outputs if they could buy them. Education and health services clearly increase an individual's productivity, and the increases are reflected in his earnings. Educated people usually earn more than uneducated people; healthy people more than sick people; and the living more than the dead. It seems reasonable to look at education and health and other social services as investments, expenditures that serve to improve the nation's productivity and the individual's earnings, which are a measure of his productive contribution. Alternative investments can thus be compared by computing the present value of the income increase that would be attributable to each and determining which promises the highest rate of return on the last dollar invested. Following this line of reasoning, economists have put a good

4. Robert Dorfman (ed.), *Measuring Benefits of Government Investments* (Brookings Institution, 1965); and Samuel B. Chase, Jr. (ed.), *Problems in Public Expenditure Analysis* (Brookings Institution, 1968).

deal of effort into estimating cost-benefit ratios for various social action programs in which the present value of future income changes is used as the measure of program benefit.

Two HEW studies used this approach in analyzing programs for disease control and manpower training.[5] The disease control study focused on several diseases for which remedies were known to be at least partially effective; it did not attempt to evaluate the benefits of research into new remedies. "Disease" was defined broadly to include injuries from motor vehicle accidents, as well as tuberculosis, syphilis, certain cancers, heart disease, and arthritis. Since programs to control each of these diseases were already in operation, the problem was to determine where additional funding would do the most good. Estimates were made of the lives that would be saved and the disabilities that would be prevented as a result of incremental expenditures on each program, and the ratio of the benefits to the costs in each program was computed.

For the killer diseases these calculations showed that, if the assumptions and guesses were right, campaigns to induce drivers to use seat belts produced relatively high ratios of lives saved per dollar expended, while tuberculosis control programs had relatively low ones.[6] This procedure valued all lives equally and ignored differences in the future productivity of the individuals whose lives would be saved.

For diseases, like arthritis, that cripple but do not kill, the problem was to find a way of comparing the benefits of preventing disability with those of preventing death, and eventually with those of other types of human investment. Another set of

5. U.S. Department of Health, Education, and Welfare, Office of the Assistant Secretary for Program Coordination, *Disease Control Programs: Selected Disease Control Programs*, Program Analysis, 1966-5 (September 1966), and *Human Investment Programs: Selected Human Investment Programs*, Program Analysis, 1966-10 (October 1966).

6. *Selected Disease Control Programs.*

benefit measures was based on estimates of the present value of additional income that would be realized through prevention of death and disability. Because estimated future income was higher for men than for women, and for those just starting their working lives than for those nearing retirement age, this procedure gave greater weight to men than to women and favored the young over the old.

A second study examined a group of training and education programs, including adult basic education, vocational education and rehabilitation, and the work-experience and training program,[7] which gave individuals education or training that might be expected to enhance their earning capacity. Again the information available on the programs was of such poor quality that it was impossible to make firm estimates of their effects on the recipients. In principle, however, the methodology of the study was straightforward benefit-cost analysis. Estimates of the earnings of recipients after the training program were compared with estimates of what their earnings would have been in its absence. The present value of the difference between the two was used as a measure of benefit in computing the ratios. Not much confidence could be placed in these ratios, but for most programs they did appear to indicate benefits well in excess of costs. Incidentally, the highest ratios of benefit to cost (about 12 or 13 to 1) were found in the program that was believed to have the most reliable data, the program for vocational rehabilitation of handicapped persons.[8]

To bring programs for younger children into this framework

7. *Selected Human Investment Programs.*

8. *Ibid.*, p. 7. Subsequent analysis of more extensive data on vocational rehabilitation confirmed these findings. U.S. Department of Health, Education, and Welfare, Office of the Assistant Secretary (Planning and Evaluation), *Human Investment Programs: Vocational Rehabilitation*, Program Analysis, 1967-13 (December 1967).

of analysis requires considerable ingenuity, since the income increases that might result are far in the future. Program results are usually stated in more immediate terms, such as reading proficiency at the end of the second grade. But analysts have found ways to approach even this problem.

Thomas Ribich, in his book, *Education and Poverty*, developed an ingenious technique for translating achievement test scores in grade school into equivalent additional years of schooling, which he then translated into equivalent income increases.[9] This technique requires a chain of heroic assumptions: that raising a child's achievement level from, say, fifth grade to sixth grade in a short time will "have the same implications for future earnings as do gains in knowledge that result from a continuation of schooling"; that "test score gains recorded in the short run will not expand or erode with the passage of time"; and that the value of additional time spent in school can be inferred from census data on the average earnings of people with differing years of schooling.[10] If these broad but not implausible assumptions are accepted, it is possible to estimate the future income increases attributable to certain school programs and to compare them with increases attributable to health and manpower training programs.

At first glance, then, benefit-cost studies seem to be pioneering efforts in a direction that might prove really useful to decision makers seeking to establish whether it would do more good to cure cancer or teach children to read. Perhaps the analysts are on the right track, and the major problem is to improve the quality and reliability of the data. With time and effort we may hope for better information on the results of reading programs,

9. Thomas I. Ribich, *Education and Poverty* (Brookings Institution, 1968), pp. 68–72.

10. *Ibid.*, p. 69.

the extent to which these results hold up as the children get older, and the actual income differences between good and bad readers. We may collect additional information on the earnings of cancer victims whose death or disability would be preventable if a cure were found. One might even expect to develop a better basis for estimating the probability that a given level of research effort on cancer would yield results.

In fact, neither HEW analysts nor any others have made much effort to refine estimates of the present value of income increases attributable to health and education programs. After the initial illustrative studies, little has been done. Are we overlooking an opportunity to improve decision making on social action programs?

Weakness of Benefit-Cost Analysis

The declining enthusiasm of the analysts for cross-program benefit-cost comparisons seems to me well founded. In the first place, as noted above, the easiest benefits for analysts to identify and measure are increases in future income. But application of this criterion to social action programs implies the acceptance of an increase in the national income as an overriding goal. It implies that this goal is more important than good health or better education or the elimination of poverty, and that these other goals are legitimate only to the extent that they increase future income. Most of us are less and less willing to accept the primacy of economic growth as an objective. As John R. Coleman, President of Haverford College, has put it:

> It is no longer self-evident that what goes up must win applause. Some costs of growth have become painfully evident: too many people, too much despoiling of the land and the lakes, too much waste left over by a careless and uncaring society. . . . True, the

economist never said it would. But the result is still that the growth goal now seems somewhat tarnished and lacking in force.[11]

Analysis based on future income ignores what most people would regard as the most important benefits of health and education. Cancer is a painful and frightening disease. People would want to be free of it even if there were no effect on future income. Reading is essential to culture and communication; it opens the doors of the mind. In their complaints about the schools, minority groups now place great emphasis on economic effects. But if such problems as irrelevant training and failure to find a job were solved, the cultural importance of reading and other educational skills would become more obvious.

While the income and economic growth benefits of social action programs will probably become less important and less interesting to decision makers over the next few years, this does not mean that it will be impossible to compare the benefits of social action programs. Ingenious analysts will be able to place shadow prices on the nonincome benefits of social action programs. But these estimates are likely to be shaky and highly judgmental. Once we leave the fairly firm ground of income we move into a kind of never-never land where we must set values on self-reliance, freedom from fear, the joys of outdoor recreation, the pleasures of clean air, and so forth. The result may not be worth the effort.

Even if we could compare the benefits of social action programs in commensurable terms, we would be left with the problem that different programs benefit different people. Social action programs typically produce both private and public benefits. The first accrue to individuals, who are, for example,

11. John R. Coleman, "Economic Understanding and Social Values—Can There Be a Consensus Any Longer?" in *Proceedings of a Symposium on Public Policy and Economic Understanding* (American Bankers Association, 1970), p. 63.

cured of cancer or taught to read; the second are diffused to others, who suffer less fear of cancer or enjoy the better life a literate society provides.[12]

The private benefits of different types of social action programs may go to entirely different groups of people. People who have cancer are not the people who cannot read. Even if we knew that the benefit-cost ratio was higher for reading programs than for cancer programs, we would not necessarily choose to devote more resources to reading. The decision would depend in part on the values attached to benefiting cancer victims and illiterates.

Although the problem of *who* should be benefited is clearly a political problem, the analyst can still help by indicating the consequences, in benefit-cost terms, of attaching different weights to the benefits flowing to various groups. For example, Thomas Ribich has suggested that, in evaluating poverty programs, greatest weight be given to the very poor.[13] He points out that a program predicated on a single poverty line would define as successful only income increases that move people across it, ignoring the size of the increase. Under these conditions, larger increases that leave families just below the line might be given lower priority. He suggests a method for arriving at a weighting system in which all income increases count, but those for the poorest count most.

Burton Weisbrod has approached the problem from the other end, suggesting that the analysts can at least show the public what implicit weights the political process attaches to benefits for different groups.[14] Where programs with lower bene-

12. See discussion in Charles L. Schultze, *The Politics and Economics of Public Spending* (Brookings Institution, 1968), pp. 83 ff.

13. Ribich, *Education and Poverty*, pp. 18–25.

14. Burton A. Weisbrod, "Income Redistribution Effects and Benefit-Cost Analysis," in Chase (ed.), *Problems in Public Expenditure Analysis*, pp. 177–209.

fit-cost ratios are chosen over those with higher ratios but different beneficiaries, Weisbrod suggests a method for estimating and displaying the advantage afforded the favored group. It is a way of saying to the politician and his constituents: "Here is what you are doing. Is this what you really meant to do?" While it seems useful, one needs great faith in the accuracy of the ratios and the identification of the beneficiaries to place much confidence in the implicit weights.

Moreover, one must also deal with the public benefits of social action programs, which are much harder to identify and to measure, though no less important, than the private benefits. Judged in terms of private benefits alone, the Salk vaccine would have been a poor national investment, since polio never attacked more than a minuscule portion of the population. Freeing the whole country from the fear and anguish it caused was clearly worth a lot, but how much? Both cancer research and literacy programs have public benefits, but it is not at all obvious how to value them. Moreover, even if ways are found to estimate these public benefits, they are not shared equally. Some people put a high subjective value on living in a literate society, and some do not. Some prize a cancer-free society, and some do not. Any decision requires weighing individual preferences against each other; while estimated dollar values may clarify the problem, only the political process can resolve it.

It is my hunch that analysts would be wasting time and effort if they gave high priority to making dollar estimates of the benefits of social action programs, for politicians and decision makers are unlikely to pay much attention to them. They and their constituents have strong, intuitive ideas about the relative importance of health, education, and social well-being that are not likely to be shaken by benefit-cost estimates. The ratios are unlikely to sway the choice of a congressman between a reading program and a cancer cure program. He is more apt to be influenced by clear statements of the benefits in physical terms, such as the number of children who will read with specified proficiency or the chances of curing certain types of cancer, and by identification of the probable beneficiaries.

When Benefit-Cost Analysis Is Useful

This discussion should not be construed as a rejection of benefit-cost analysis, nor as an attempt to downgrade the importance of defining and measuring the benefits of social action programs. On the contrary, as Chapter 2 pointed out, one of the most important contributions of the analysts to decision making has been the greater precision about what is being bought and for whom. The sensible decision between cancer and reading programs requires knowledge of who will read better, what effect this greater skill might have on their lives, who is likely to escape death and disability from cancer, and what the consequences might be. Moreover, measures of the outputs of social action programs are essential to the analysis of the relative effectiveness of various ways of producing them (see Chapters 4 and 5). Finally, such measurements act to hold the managers of social action programs accountable to their clients and to create incentives for more effective management (see Chapter 6). If these benefits or outputs can be easily stated in dollars, so much the better. The only thing rejected here is a substantial effort to make the benefits of various social action programs commensurable in dollar terms. Such comparisons seem not only likely to be shaky but unrewarding, since distributional considerations dominate the decision.

Straightforward benefit-cost analysis, and strenuous efforts to place a monetary value on the benefits and compare them, are, however, clearly justified when the programs under consideration are primarily investment programs, designed to increase future income. The justification is especially valid when the decision involves alternative ways of increasing the income of the same people. Two examples of decision problems illustrate the relevance and usefulness of traditional benefit-cost analysis.

The first is a classic decision between alternative dam sites. Here the primary justification for building the dam is investment in the production of cheaper electric power, although other benefits, such as flood control and outdoor recreation, may also accrue. In this instance, evaluation of these other benefits in dollar terms and comparisons of the benefit-cost ratios of the two projects seem helpful. The distributional problem would remain, of course, for the beneficiaries of the two are not the same. The political process may lead to the choice of the project with the lower benefit-cost ratio. But as long as the primary justification of the project is its contribution to economic growth, the ratios are clearly relevant.

In the social action area, benefit-cost analysis aids the choice between income maintenance and various types of human investment as routes out of poverty for the same people. Consider, for example, alternative policies with respect to recipients of aid to dependent children, who are mostly mothers with children, although unemployed fathers are present in some cases. The objective is to provide an adequate income and improve the prospects of productive lives for the children. One policy is straight income maintenance, which might be regarded as paying mothers to look after their own children. Given the number and size of the families and the level of payments, estimating the cost of this policy is fairly straightforward. The alternative policy is to encourage mothers to work by offering them training opportunities, job placement services, and day care for their children. It is much more difficult to estimate what this will cost and what family incomes will result. To develop such estimates requires assumptions about the proportions of mothers who will voluntarily seek training, stick with it, and obtain a job; about their earnings, above the costs incurred by working; about the duration of their employment; and about the costs of day care. With reasonable faith in these assumptions, one can compare the expected incomes of the families and the cost to the government of the alternative approaches.

The choice of one policy over the other, however, should not turn on the relation of future incomes to cost alone. Those who put a high value on self-sufficiency might choose training, work, and day care even if this approach were more costly. The effects of the two policies on the children are also important. The day care experience could have educational benefits for the children that might be reaped in school or later work. Separation from their mothers might also be detrimental, at least to some children. These effects should be estimated, if possible, and weighed in the decision.

In an effort to set budget levels for the work incentive (WIN) program, HEW in 1968 made such a comparison (which, however, ignored the effects on children). Despite rather conservative assumptions about the proportion of mothers who would become self-supporting and rather generous allowances for day care, the study indicated that training, work, and day care would probably mean net savings for the federal budget after any one group of mothers had been in the program five to six years.[15] In the initial years, the work policy was more costly than straight income maintenance because the training and day care costs were heavy.

15. U.S. Department of Health, Education, and Welfare, Office of the Assistant Secretary (Planning and Evaluation), *Program Memorandum on Income Maintenance and Social and Rehabilitation Services Programs of DHEW, Fiscal Years 1970–1974* (November 1968), p. II.19.

This computation of benefits and costs of training welfare recipients was a useful, if speculative, piece of benefit-cost analysis. Its weakness lay in the lack of solid analysis of the costs of providing effective training and day care, and in the absence of a firm basis for predicting the behavior of individuals in the face of training and employment opportunities. Subsequent chapters are concerned with these types of problems.

4 Producing Effective Services: What Do We Know?

How much have the analysts helped those who want to make better decisions on social action programs? The last chapter gave them low marks. They have not progressed very far toward making the benefits of social action programs comparable, nor can they offer much help with the larger issue of how to allocate public resources among major types of programs.

This chapter addresses a different question: If the analysts cannot say how much to spend for health or education, can they at least say how to produce particular kinds of health or education more effectively?

Again the answer is discouraging. So far the analysts can provide little useful information about the relative effectiveness of various educational methods or health delivery systems. Moreover, there is scant analytical basis for predicting the behavior of individuals and families in response to changes in incentives or availability of new services.

Unfortunately, these shortcomings matter. Without knowing how to produce more effective services or how people will respond to changes in social policy, analysts cannot contribute much to decision making for social action.

This chapter will attempt to explain the failure to progress in evaluating different ways of producing social services. The fault does not lie entirely with the analysts: They must have something to analyze, and neither social service delivery systems nor government programs are organized to generate information about their effectiveness. Furthermore, new techniques or combinations of resources are not tried out systematically so that their effectiveness can be evaluated. Until programs are organized so that analysts can learn from them and systematic experimentation is undertaken on a significant scale, prospects seem dim for learning how to produce better social services.

Why Do We Care?

Why is the nation suddenly concerned about the effectiveness of social services? After all, people got along for centuries without explicitly measuring the effectiveness of education, health service delivery, and other social services. Dedicated individuals ran schools and hospitals and dispensed charity to the needy. As various theories of teaching or treatment or hospital organization were advanced from time to time, people put them into practice, and techniques of service changed over the years. Resources were allocated in response to perceived needs, changes in costs, and political pressure. Somehow we muddled through.

Now dissatisfaction with social services runs very high indeed. Much of the concern centers on the fragmentation and apparent ineffectiveness of training programs, job placement, urban renewal, and other special services for the poor. But dissatisfaction with social services is not confined to the poor. Many students, for example, believe that colleges and universities are not well organized to educate them for modern life. Many professors agree, and President Nixon has explained the low priority given education funds in the budget on the grounds that American education has to be reformed before it can use more resources effectively.[1] That the system for delivering health services is outmoded and must be reorganized to serve more effectively rich and poor alike has become a cliché.

Economists, of course, have always had theoretical reasons for questioning the organization of public services. In general, they are produced under monopolistic conditions. The consumer can rarely shop around among public schools or hospitals or welfare departments. Even if he could, he would have scant information by which to measure and judge the quality of health

1. "American Education—Message from the President of the United States," *Congressional Record*, daily ed., March 3, 1970, pp. H1405–09.

or education or other social services. Conservatives have always made these points in arguing for less public activity and more reliance on the private market. But more recently, the liberals, who generally favor *more* public activity, have been among the sharpest critics of public services. What has happened? Have America's social services all at once deteriorated?

The available evidence, albeit superficial, gives no reason to suspect a general deterioration. Doctors, nurses, teachers, and social workers are better trained. Medical science has advanced rapidly. Although schools, hospitals, and other physical facilities have deteriorated in some neighborhoods, most are more elaborately equipped than ever before. The average American is probably getting better education and health care and social services than his parents did.

While social services have, if anything, improved, two other developments have affected our assessment of them: Aspirations have shifted from quantity to quality and we have a new perception of our ignorance about quality.

It is hard to focus on too many aspirations at once. For many years the nation emphasized simple access to social services for those who needed them. With the great progress that has been made toward this goal, aspirations have shifted to performance. For years, policy makers were concerned with building and staffing more schools to keep pace with the population increase, with keeping children in school more years by lowering dropout rates, eliminating double shifts, and adding kindergarten or preschool—in short, with how to provide enough education, not how to make it better. To the extent that they were concerned with quality, they focused on giving children access to schools that met minimum standards—getting rid of the one-room school house, the outdoor privy, and the uncertified teacher; or making sure that lunchrooms, gymnasiums, libraries, and science labs were available to a larger number of children. But access is not enough. Children go to school but do not learn. We must find ways to make education more effective.

The process of achieving universal access has in itself revealed how ineffective social service systems are when they have to produce for everybody. Only a few years ago, most people thought that the nation's medical care system—with its public and private hospitals, and doctors, mostly in private practice, operating on a fee-for-service basis—was functioning reasonably well. Not everyone was delighted with the system, but the main problem seemed to be that so many people were excluded from it simply because they could not pay. To solve the problem, medicare and medicaid put purchasing power into the hands of the old and many of the poor, but made no attempt to change the delivery system itself.

The result was to intensify the pressure on a fairly stable supply of resources already staggering under the impact of a rapid increase in demand. Demand for medical care was increasing for many reasons: growing population, higher incomes, widening private insurance coverage, increasing faith in the efficacy of medical treatment. The supply of medical services increases relatively slowly because it takes a long time to train a doctor or build a health facility, because the medical profession has strict rules about who can do what, and because the technology is ever more complex and expensive. There was little incentive to use the existing supply of medical services more efficiently. Indeed, the prevalence of hospital insurance both encouraged the use of hospitals and relieved them of pressure from patients to keep costs down.

As any student of elementary economics could have predicted, a rapid price increase ensued.[2] To extend access to medical care

2. For a discussion of the medical price increases of the mid-1960s, see U.S. Department of Health, Education, and Welfare, *A Report to the President on Medical Care Prices* (1967).

without changing the system is to incur higher prices for everybody. The magnitudes involved are so staggering that they have forced the government and even the profession to ask whether there is a better way of organizing medical services. Perhaps some of the things doctors do could be done by less-skilled personnel. Maybe preventive medicine, or treatment at home or in extended care facilities, could relieve hospitals of some of the burden. Maybe payment mechanisms could be improved to provide incentives for cost control.

Higher education also seemed to work well for the relatively small proportion of the population who had access to it. The variety of institutions—some public, some private; some with high standards, many with low ones—appeared adequate to their perceived needs. There were a few large universities, but the typical student was in a small college. Colleges and universities dispensed knowledge and culture mainly to the middle class. The poor youngster with guts and determination could work his way through, but he had to have middle-class aspirations and motivations.

The present crisis in higher education is not simple, but it is at least partly a result of the attempt to extend the higher education system, which worked well for the few, to a much larger group, with far more diverse aspirations, motivations, and experience, studying in much larger institutions. One result is a new level of concern with the effectiveness of higher education and a new search for alternative ways of organizing the process.

Those who cared about better education, health, and social services have, until recently, thought the main problem was underfinancing. They thought far too much was spent on the private sector and far too little on public needs. They were confident that an influx of resources into the public sector—for example, federal aid to education—would produce results. But the answer is not a simplistic "Spend more money." Even the liberals are no longer sure they would know what to do if they had more to spend for social services, or that it would do much good.

I am not alleging that the *level* of ignorance about how to produce effective services has increased. Firm information never existed. But five years ago, heedless of their ignorance, liberals were earnestly fighting for increases in federal aid to education or health. What has changed is our *perception* of our ignorance. We now know that we do not know.

The analysts who have addressed themselves to the problems of producing social services have been partially responsible for exposing this ignorance. They have raised new questions, and revealed the lack of answers. Unfortunately, they have not yet made much progress toward finding the answers.

Learning from the System

Education provides a good example of the problems involved in analysis of the production of a social service. Although economists and statisticians have paid attention to education only since the mid-sixties, they have already written a substantial literature and uncovered a lot of pitfalls. Many of the same problems occur in analyzing health care and other social services.

The analysis of the education process rests on two premises. The first is that at least some of the important outcomes of education are identifiable and measurable. Reading skills, mathematical proficiency, and acquired knowledge of certain subjects can be approximated by test scores. These test scores are, of course, imperfect proxies for intellectual skills that are themselves merely means to effective functioning later in life; moreover, they are by no means the only desirable products of the school experience. Nevertheless, it does not seem unreasonable to focus on these measurable outcomes, and see what light analysis can throw on how best to produce them. The second premise is that fairly stable relationships exist between these outcomes and the "inputs" to the educational process: different types of teachers, facilities, equipment, curriculum, and teaching methods. Of course, this premise may be false. All methods of teaching may be equally effective or ineffective. The ratio of teachers to pupils, the training of teachers, the kind of building, may have absolutely no influence on what students learn. However, this seems unlikely. A reasonable working hypothesis holds that education influences learning in some regular and discoverable way, that education has, in economists' jargon, a "production function"—some functional relationship between the types and proportions of resources used and the results produced.

At the moment, systems analysts seeking to discover the relationships between inputs and outputs and techniques in education have two major sources of information: One is the education system itself; the other is evaluation of special projects or programs, especially those financed by the federal government.

Elementary and Secondary Education

When economists and other analysts first became interested in education, they found it reasonable to start by examining the system and identifying more and less efficient ways of producing education. Tens of thousands of school districts and hundreds of thousands of schools produced education with different levels of resources, different types of buildings and teachers and curricula, and different results. It seemed reasonable to use this "natural experiment" to uncover some stable relationships among the inputs, the outputs, and the technologies.

There were even some data. Many cities and some states

collect achievement test scores, dropout rates, and other measures of the output of their school systems, and can provide accounting and other information on the characteristics of buildings, teachers, and other inputs. Moreover, in the last decade, two major national surveys, Project TALENT and the Survey of Educational Opportunity, known as the Coleman Report, have collected both output and input information on a large sample of schools.[3]

Many analysts have worked over these statistics, attempting to find regular relationships between the inputs and the outputs. Kiesling sought to relate test scores and other output data to resource information for a sample of New York communities, while Burkhead analyzed data for Chicago, Atlanta, and a group of smaller communities. Shaycoft, Ribich, and others tried to discover relations between inputs and outputs in the Project TALENT survey. Coleman, and later Mayeske and others, subjected the Survey of Educational Opportunity to intensive analysis.[4] Those who wrote the studies and those who

3. John C. Flanagan and others, *Project TALENT*, a survey conducted by the University of Pittsburgh for the U.S. Office of Education in 1960, whose results have been published in a number of volumes by the University of Pittsburgh, 1960–64; and James S. Coleman and others, *Equality of Educational Opportunity*, U.S. Department of Health, Education, and Welfare (1966).

4. Herbert J. Kiesling, "The Relationship of School Inputs to Public School Performance in New York State," P-4211 (RAND Corporation, 1969; processed); Jesse Burkhead, with Thomas G. Fox and John W. Holland, *Input and Output in Large-City High Schools* (Syracuse University Press, 1967); Marion F. Shaycoft, *The High School Years: Growth in Cognitive Skills* (University of Pittsburgh, American Institutes for Research and School of Education, 1967; processed); Thomas I. Ribich, *Education and Poverty* (Brookings Institution, 1968); the Coleman Report; and George W. Mayeske and others, "A Study of Our Nation's Schools," U.S. Department of Health, Education, and Welfare, Office of Education (1969; processed). For an interesting use of the Coleman data and comprehensive references to data sources, see Samuel Bowles, "Towards an Educational Production Function," in W. Lee Hansen (ed.), *Education, Income, and Human Capital* (Columbia University Press for the National Bureau of Economic Research, 1970), pp. 11–61.

read them would all probably admit to disappointment in the results. No clear patterns emerge. Few prescriptions can be given for improving the effectiveness of schools.

One major conclusion shows up in all these studies: Variations in school inputs have limited power to explain differences in student performance. In none of these studies did variables such as class size or age of building or teacher training, *taken together*, explain much of the variation in student performance; the socioeconomic status of the students themselves and of their schoolmates mattered more. This result suggests that the school performance of students might be improved by increasing the income, education, housing, or employment of their parents. It also suggests that racial and economic integration may help. In schools in which the majority was white or of at least moderate income, black and lower-income children appeared to do better, while the majority children did no worse.[5]

For the school administrator who must take the socioeconomic mix of his students as given, however, the results are discouraging. He has to ask: "How can I affect educational performance by changing school characteristics?" And these statistical studies appear to answer: "No matter what you do, you can't affect school performance much." The firmness of this conclusion should not be exaggerated, however. In the first place, as Bowles and Levin have pointed out, some statistical procedures tend to exaggerate the effect of the socioeconomic variables.[6] The socioeconomic variables and the resource vari-

5. *Racial Isolation in the Public Schools*, A Report of the U.S. Commission on Civil Rights (1967).

6. Samuel S. Bowles and Henry M. Levin, "The Determinants of Scholastic Achievement: An Appraisal of Some Recent Evidence," *Journal of Human Resources*, Vol. 3 (Winter 1968), pp. 3–24 (Brookings Reprint 145); and Bowles and Levin, "More on Multicollinearity and the Effectiveness of Schools," *Journal of Human Resources*, Vol. 3 (Summer 1968), pp. 393–400; James S.

ables tend to be positively correlated with each other—richer students go to better-endowed schools—a fact significant in itself. This makes it hard to separate statistically the effect of socioeconomic status from the effect of resources.

Moreover, all of the studies show some positive correlations between resources and performance, and, taken together, they support the contention that resources count. In a study made for the Urban Coalition in support of a court action to equalize educational expenditures in the state of Michigan, Guthrie and his colleagues brought together in one table all the significant positive correlations between inputs and school performance established in these studies.[7] While a court might well be convinced by this evidence that resources are positively related to educational performance, a superintendent of schools or commissioner of education would not be much enlightened. He already knew resources were important. He needs help in how to spend them.

Even when a significant positive relation is found between school performance and some school input, the relationship is generally weak. Indeed, the analyst is pleased to find that there is any relationship at all and that it has the "right" sign. He is pleased when the statistical analysis confirms—however tenuously—what he thought he knew anyway! When the analysis fails to confirm his preconceptions—when the coefficients have the "wrong" sign—he suspects he has made a mistake. At least he is cautious about giving advice. In Burkhead's Atlanta study, dropout rates turned out to be *positively* correlated with

---

Coleman, "The Concept of Equality of Educational Opportunity," *Harvard Educational Review*, Vol. 38 (Winter 1968), pp. 7–22.

7. James W. Guthrie and others, "Schools and Inequality: A Study of Social Status, School Services, Student Performance, and Post-School Opportunity in Michigan" (Urban Coalition, 1969; processed).

expenditures. His cautious conclusion was: "The high positive association of current expenditures and dropout rates would suggest that simply allocating more resources will not help this problem."[8] The superintendent of schools in Atlanta might well wonder if he should take resources away. "Simply allocating more resources" was not one of his options anyway. Resources have to be spent in some particular way, and the correlation does not indicate whether specific programs would reduce dropouts or not.

The studies as a group do not indicate which inputs should be increased relative to others. Measures of teacher quality, such as verbal ability or teacher's salary, appear significant more frequently than other measures, but this is hardly more than a confirmation of the conventional wisdom in education.[9] Most people suspected that teachers were important in education.

Why do the analysts not find stronger and clearer relationships between school inputs and performance of children?

First, most of these studies were based on measurements that show the relationship between school variables and the performance of children in a single year. One would hardly expect a cumulative process like education to produce strong relationships between inputs and outputs in a single year. Children do a lot of moving around among schools and school systems, and even the child who stays in the same school may have a good teacher one year and a poor teacher the next. It is his cumulative experience that affects his performance and that should be expected to show up in test scores and other measures. A study that related a child's school experience over several years to

8. Burkhead and others, *Input and Output*, p. 72.

9. Henry M. Levin, "A Cost-Effectiveness Analysis of Teacher Selection," *Journal of Human Resources*, Vol. 5 (Winter 1970), pp. 24–33; U.S. Department of Health, Education, and Welfare, Office of Education, "Do Teachers Make A Difference?" A Report on Recent Research on Pupil Achievement (1970).

changes in his performance over the longer period might reveal strong relationships between the two even though the single-year relationships were weak.

Second, the output measures may be poor ones. A test may not be a valid measure of what the students have learned, either because it is poorly constructed or because the test-takers do not care whether they do well on it. The tests may be inadequate to measure what some schools are teaching. If some schools emphasize skills that others ignore, then the relationship between school variables and the results of any one set of tests might be expected to be weak. Moreover, tests that purport to measure skills acquired in school may actually be measuring native ability. Here again a measure of change over time, rather than of level in a single year, would help by filtering out the native ability factor and would come closer to being a measure of learning acquired in school.

Third, while the analysts knew they were using proxies for more basic variables, they may have chosen poorly. The age of the school building is probably not nearly as important as the arrangement of its rooms. The number of volumes in the library is presumably not as crucial as the choice of books and their accessibility. A teacher's score on a verbal test may not matter as much as her sympathy, her sense of humor, or her confidence in her students.

Fourth, even if the inputs and outputs are accurately measured and a relationship among them actually exists, it may be hard to find with the statistical methods used. Variation in actual schools may be too small to allow big differences to emerge. Classes are all about the same size; curriculum, teaching methods, even types of buildings, do not vary much. Perhaps radical departures from existing patterns would produce very different results. Suppose, for example, that class size makes little difference for classes of from twenty to forty students, but a marked improvement in learning occurs when class size falls from twenty to ten. If almost all the statistics came from classes of twenty to forty, they would not give correct estimates of the impact of shifting to much smaller class sizes. Suppose, further, that it is possible to improve student performance in a small class only by changing the way in which the teacher spends her time. The teacher may not know this or may not want to try it. Hence, even if there are small classes in the sample, the statistical relationship between class size and performance will not reflect what would be possible if everyone knew about the most effective techniques and were willing to use them. Furthermore, the relationship between inputs and outputs may vary with different types of children. If it were true, for example, that smart children learn more easily in big classes and slow children in small ones, then the relationship between class size and learning might appear to be weak when estimates were based on a sample of both types of children mixed together.

Fifth, in most of these studies, the unit of observation was not the child, but the school or the classroom. Even where the observational unit appeared to be the child, he was generally assumed to have the same access to the resources provided as all other children in his grade or school. Within a school or classroom, one child may get considerably more attention or resources than another, and averaging these out may mask a real relationship between inputs and outputs.

For all these reasons, it is not surprising that the statistical studies undertaken so far have failed to reveal close relationships between school inputs and outputs, granting they exist.

What would it take to do a better job? Assuming a production function—that is, some fairly stable relationships between the quantity and quality of the inputs and the curriculum and methods, and the results—and assuming enough variation in the "natural experiment" so that we can discover something about the shape of this function, we need at least three things: (1) a longitudinal data system for keeping track of individual children as they move through school and for recording changes in their performance; (2) detailed program information and resource information at the level of the individual child to reveal, for example, not just whether he was in a school that had a remedial reading program, but how many hours he has been in the program and what kind of a program it was; (3) information on the child's own characteristics and family background to be taken into consideration in assessing the effects of the school on the child.

This kind of intensive longitudinal analysis of education has not been tried on a major scale, but it ought to be. The technology is available. It is possible to follow children as they move through a school system and even into other school systems. It is possible to store and retrieve a great deal of information on performance of individual children over time and on the programs in which they have participated.

In view of the potential usefulness of these kinds of data it is surprising that more school systems are not collecting, storing, and analyzing them. Some are beginning to do so. The District of Columbia, for example, is giving earnest consideration to a longitudinal data bank.[10] But most school systems still use test information mainly for individual diagnostic purposes, not for program evaluation, and fail to collect or use cumulative information on children's school experience.

I am *not* saying that bodies of data like the Coleman study and Project TALENT should not have been collected or should not have been analyzed for their illumination of the relation-

10. H. R. Cort, Jr., with Mildred P. Cooper, "Evaluation of Programs in the D.C. Public Schools—Some Strategies and Systems," Final Report (Washington School of Psychiatry, February 1970; processed).

ships between educational inputs and outputs. With all their limitations—the inadequate input and output measures, the single-year cross-section—they afforded a chance to uncover something interesting and helpful. More complex and expensive longitudinal studies would not have been justified until the existing data had been thoroughly analyzed. But the limitations of these studies are not well understood. Laymen and even public officials interpret their results as proving that "nothing works in education" or as pointing to the even less warranted conclusion that "nothing *could* work in education."

Moreover, the results of intensive longitudinal analysis may not turn out to be much more conclusive than the superficial cross-sectional studies. The problem may be that the real world is not organized to generate information about production functions, no matter how cleverly the statistics are collected. Perhaps the schools are too uniform, with too few important differences that are not correlated with the socioeconomic status of students. It may be necessary deliberately to experiment with radically different curricula, mixes of resources, or approaches before any significant differences in outcome emerge (see Chapter 5). Experimentation is so expensive, however, that a major effort should be made to learn from the natural experiment wherever possible.

Higher Education

The situation is no better in higher education than in elementary and secondary schooling. Analytical studies so far have simply not yielded much useful information about relationships between inputs and outputs.

No comprehensive attempt has been made to relate inputs to outputs in higher education, in part because it seems harder to measure output at this level than in elementary or secondary school. Some studies have identified outputs with changes in student test scores over the college period (using scholastic aptitude tests for freshmen and graduate record examinations for seniors).[11] In results analogous to those at the elementary and secondary levels, not much of the variance in test score changes can be explained by standard resource measures such as buildings, or library books, or faculty ratios or salaries or degrees. Stronger relationships exist between individual score changes and the average score of the rest of the college. In other words, your fellow students may make more difference than the resources of your college.

The inability of the analysts to point up the most effective ways to produce higher education may also be attributed to the problems discussed above. Measures of input and output and of resources are all shaky. Individual students within a single institution are exposed to vastly different mixes of resources, and these differences tend to be averaged out in the statistical studies. Moreover, real differences among institutions are not great: Most college catalogues look pretty much alike. Innovations occur sporadically, but no systematic experiments with radical changes in methods or mixes of resources are carried out or evaluated. The system is simply not organized to generate information that would tell us how to produce higher education more effectively.

Learning from Federal Programs

If it is so hard to analyze usefully the education systems themselves, what can one learn from federal programs designed to

11. For a good review of this literature see Robert H. Berls, "An Exploration of the Determinants of Effectiveness in Higher Education," in *The Economics and Financing of Higher Education in the United States*, A Compendium of Papers Submitted to the Joint Economic Committee, 91 Cong. 1 sess. (1969), pp. 207–60.

increase the effectiveness of education? Unfortunately, not much. And the reasons are clear: The programs were not designed with this purpose in view. Title I of the Elementary and Secondary Education Act of 1965 is a good example.

Title I, which provided about $1 billion a year to school districts for special projects to improve the education of poor or educationally deprived children, was passed largely on faith. That educated people are less likely to be poor and that children from poor families tend to perform badly in school were known facts. That extra resources spent to "compensate" for lack of intellectual stimulation at home would improve the performance of poor children in school and break the cycle of poverty was a tenet of faith. No one really knew *how* to run a successful compensatory education program. There were hunches and theories, but few facts. The decision was to provide funds to local education systems for special programs for poor children. The educator hoped for significant improvements in the average performance of poor children. The analyst hoped that something would be learned from the experience. Both have been largely disappointed.

In 1966, as activity under Title I got under way, expectations were high both for the program and for its useful evaluation. The districts got very little guidance on how to spend the money, partly because the Congress wanted to avoid the appearance of federal control and partly because no one knew what guidance to give. The money was spent in a wide variety of ways: special reading programs, after-school tutoring, math programs, cultural enrichment, breakfast programs, and so forth. To an analyst not yet discouraged by lack of results in cross-sectional surveys, analysis of this natural experiment appeared likely to uncover something about what worked and what did not. Couldn't we measure success in some way—changes in test scores, dropout rates, attitudes, and so forth—and see whether success thus measured was associated in some regular way with level of resources per child, age of child, or type of program? It seemed logical at the time.

The first step was to gather together some distinguished educators and systems analysts to talk over the problem. That first meeting established only that they do not speak the same language. The educators were frightened by words like "input" and "output" and "production function," and the systems analysts did not understand their fear. But the effort persisted and funds were finally provided for several studies of the relationship between inputs and outputs in compensatory education projects. One of these, a contract with TEMPO, a division of General Electric, is worth a detailed discussion, not because it was so important, but because it illustrates so well the difficulties of this type of study.[12]

For TEMPO, a pilot study on a small scale, fourteen fairly big cities were selected, not randomly, but because they had functioning Title I programs and were willing to cooperate. Teams composed of department and contractor staff went out to dig out information from a sample of participating schools. In the end, data from only eleven cities were suitable for analysis.

It was immediately clear that it was impossible to look at the effectiveness of Title I by itself, since similar programs not financed by federal money were also in progress. The effectiveness of compensatory education for poor children had to be scrutinized. However, two years were chosen—1965–66, the year before there was any substantial Title I activity and 1966–67, the first full year of Title I—and an attempt was made to

12. E. J. Mosbaek and others, "Analyses of Compensatory Education in Five School Districts: Summary" (Santa Barbara, Calif.: General Electric Company, TEMPO, 1968; processed).

measure changes between them and to relate these changes to level and type of compensatory education activity.

No uniform test was possible because national testing, besides being expensive, is a bugaboo of school people. Hence it was necessary to rely on test score information available in the systems themselves, along with information on other outputs, like dropout rates. Moreover, test scores could not be obtained for the same children in successive years because most school systems do not test the same children every year. They generally test the same grades—the first, fourth, and seventh grades, for example—so test score measures were used on the same grade in two successive years. Since these were poverty area schools, mobility among schools was extremely high; in some cases, fewer than half the students had been in the same school the previous year.

Information on resources devoted to compensatory education was even scantier. Most school systems keep central books and have no reliable means of estimating the resources devoted to a particular grade and a particular school. Estimates of the type and magnitude of compensatory education provided to particular grades were obtained with great effort, and, at that, in only a few cities.

The results of this effort were not spectacular. Wide variation appeared in the test scores between the two years. Some went up, some went down. For the sample as a whole, on the average, there was a slight decline in test scores between the two years, perhaps attributable to the changing population of the schools. Consistent with the casual observation of the analysts that a high proportion of the resources was going to the least able students, a slight increase occurred in the test scores of the lowest decile. Where program type and resource level could be linked with test changes, no significant association emerged, except for a suggestion in some cities that concentrating resources in larger blocs helps.

The study incidentally illustrated another hazard: too much publicity. As soon as they got wind of this rather modest study, reporters from a number of newspapers began inquiring about results. As a condition for the school system's cooperation, promises had been made to guard information that would reveal the identity of the city, but some reporters suspected a bureaucratic plot to withhold information. When the study was completed and its results released, newsmen jumped on the fact that the average test scores between the two years had not increased and the headlines read, "U.S. Priming of School 'Pumps' Fails To Raise Learning Level."[13] Many of those involved spent days on the phone explaining to congressmen, their aides, and others that the study did not show that at all; that it was a limited sample; that it was only for one year; that the test scores were not for the same children; that many of the children tested had not had any special services, and so on. But few were interested in the explanations.

In fact, the TEMPO study did not show anything at all, one way or another, about Title I. It showed only how hard it is to find out anything about input-output relations in education, especially from a quick, low-budget project using existing data. Unfortunately, however, it also added to the layman's impression that "compensatory education doesn't work" and led some to believe that "there is nothing we can do through education that will help poor children."

The main problem was not the study; it was the design of the Title I program. Even from a better study with uniform testing

13. Story by Philip Meyer, Chicago Daily News Service, which appeared in newspapers around the country, Jan. 8, 1969. A similar article by Peter Milius of *The Washington Post* appeared in several papers Jan. 2, 1969.

of the same children in different years, and more adequate descriptions of compensatory programs and of the resources devoted to them, we still might not have learned much, because the program simply was not designed to yield information on effectiveness. There was no experimental design. There were no control groups. There was no attempt to define promising methods or approaches and try them out in enough places to test their operation under different conditions. Moreover, in most places the additional resources devoted to Title I children were too limited to have supported hope of finding effects that would stand out clearly over those of other school and nonschool factors.

Headstart, another program undertaken with a hunch and a prayer, offers an even better example of a missed opportunity to learn from a social action program. Often unused to talking and listening, especially to middle-class speech, and unable to deal easily with shapes and colors and numerical concepts, poor children were known to start school at a disadvantage. Perhaps they lost confidence in the first year and never regained it. Perhaps something could be done to give them a "head start," to bring them up to the level of middle-class children and to overcome the initial handicaps that were hampering their progress.

Headstart was conceived and started with remarkable rapidity. An appealing idea, it caught the imagination of Congress and the public. Everyone wanted to move ahead fast. There were varying ideas about what kind of program was appropriate, what ages were best for it, how long it should last. In effect, local Headstart projects were free, within budgetary limits, to try any approach that seemed reasonable. Tremendous political pressure was exerted to involve more children in short summer programs rather than fewer children in more expensive all-year programs.

After the fact, an evaluation attempted to uncover whether the program had had an *average* effect, discernible in test scores at the first and second grade levels. But the program was not designed to answer the really important and interesting questions: Were some approaches more successful than others? Were some more successful with particular types of children?

Why was this opportunity missed? First, it is tremendously difficult to design and manage good experiments. The experimenter incurs administrative headaches, besides charges of interference with local initiative and of using innocent children as guinea pigs. Money has to be allocated to administration and evaluation that could be used to serve more children. But the failure to design programs so that something can be learned from them may be due to lack of courage on the part of administrators and social scientists. They are afraid to admit that they do not know. And they may be wise. The Office of Economic Opportunity might have told Congress: "We don't know whether preschool programs will work, or what kind would be best, but we have designed a program to find out." But would they then have gotten the money?

5 Can We Find Out What Works?

If the reader has accepted the argument of the last chapter, he must be discouraged. It started from two premises: that education, health, and other social services are not effectively produced now, and that some techniques or forms of organization or combinations of resources now in use are probably more effective than others—if we could only find out what they are. It concluded that so far the efforts of systems analysts to identify these better methods have met with little success.

One reason that not much has been learned from statistical analysis of the existing health, education, and social service systems may be inadequate description of inputs and outputs, and lack of information on the same individuals over time. Another is the failure thus far to organize social service systems to facilitate investigation of their effectiveness. Major deviations from the established pattern are rare and their effects are hard to disentangle from the special circumstances that brought them about. Equally little has been learned from evaluation of federal government programs. The reasons are much the same. Headstart, Title I, model cities, and other federal programs *could* have been designed to produce information on their effectiveness, but they were not.

What can be done? The last chapter recommended intensified efforts to learn from the "natural experiment" created by the regular system and by federal programs. It emphasized the importance of longitudinal information and the application of more sophisticated statistical techniques. This chapter will recommend an additional strategy, not incompatible with the first. It will argue that the federal government should take the leadership in organizing, funding, and evaluating systematic experiments with various ways of delivering education, health, and other social services. The strategy involves several steps. The first is a major effort to identify new teaching methods, new ways of organizing or paying for health services, or new types of income transfer systems that show promise of increasing effectiveness. The second calls for *systematically* trying out new methods in various places and under various conditions. The final step is the evaluation of new methods under different conditions and their comparison with each other and with methods already in use. These experiments should be carefully designed, on a large enough scale and with sufficient controls to permit valid conclusions about the relative effectiveness of various methods.

Systematic experimentation is a radical new strategy of social reform. The key word is "systematic." "Experiment" has been loosely used in recent years as a synonym for "new" or "innovative." Government and foundations have promoted hundreds of "experimental" programs, but no one has been following a strategy of systematic experimentation. Indeed, the strategy of the 1960s is more aptly described as "random innovation."

The first part of this chapter will discuss the differences between random innovation and systematic experimentation. The rest will deal with some concrete examples of systematic experiments and with some arguments for and against the adoption of this strategy.

Random Innovation

"Random innovation" describes a strategy in which individual communities or schools or health facilities are encouraged to try new approaches and see how they work. The rationale is simple: Bureaucracy stifles innovation; "change agents" must be found and fostered if the services are to become more effective.

In an education or health system, an inevitable and continuous conflict arises between administrative rules and innovation. The rules are usually imposed for good reasons—to insure that only qualified doctors minister to patients and qualified teachers to students, that dangerous medicines are subject to proper control and essential parts of the curriculum are taught. Nevertheless, the more rules and standards and guidelines, the greater the tendency to stifle new and possibly more effective ways of delivering services.

Yet despite a plethora of regulations, scope for innovation does exist. The decentralization of social services in the United States leaves considerable room for random innovation at the local level. There is, after all, no national curriculum for the schools, no national system of delivering or even paying for health services, no national standard for payments or services to the needy. In general, the innovator does not have to change the whole country at once or confront a national bureaucracy. In fact, exceptional teachers and creative school principals try new methods and approaches all the time. Innovative health officers or hospital administrators reorganize their institutions, experiment with new staffing patterns, new concepts of neighborhood, ambulatory, or outpatient care. The country is dotted with imaginative nursery schools, clinics, training programs, community action projects of all kinds.

In the 1960s the federal government sought to foster this random innovation as its major strategy in the social action area. The premise was that there were people out there with good ideas who needed only money and encouragement to produce more effective services. The community action program was a prime example of this strategy, the model cities program another. A third was Title III of the Elementary and Secondary Education Act, whose guidelines were, in effect, "Try something new." Title I of the same act can also be regarded as primarily an invitation to random innovation. While it specified a detailed formula for distributing the money to school districts with children from low-income families, neither the law nor the federal guidelines said much about how these "educationally deprived" children were to be helped.

The random innovation strategy of the 1960s produced tens of thousands of "innovative projects." Some were wasteful or foolish; many simply increased the level of services delivered in much the same way; some were genuinely new and more effective. But most, including some of the more successful ones, never received national publicity. No one knows about them except the participants and the immediate community. Often they were unevaluated. The people who worked in them may have known they did a good job, but no visible evidence or measurable statistics emerged that would convince someone else.

This state of affairs suggests that the random innovation strategy lacked a final stage—the dissemination of results. Perhaps the federal government should divert some of its funds for random innovation to finding and describing successful projects, distributing literature, making films, holding workshops and training sessions to spread the word. But the difficulty in selecting exemplary projects for publicity is that each one is unique. Nobody is sure how relevant a successful program will be to other circumstances and other areas. Is its success attributable to a specially gifted teacher or a charismatic doctor or administrator? Were the participants self-selected and perhaps more highly motivated than other people? Was there a Hawthorne effect, that is, were the results influenced by the simple fact that something new was done?[1] In the absence of a sys-

1. The term originated from a study of the effect of monotony on workers, made at the Hawthorne Works of the Western Electric Company in Chicago between 1927 and 1932. It was found that when management paid attention—no matter what kind—to workers, output increased. For example, decreasing illumi-

tematic effort to try out the new approach under a variety of circumstances, or to try parts of it separately and together, no one really knows what to publicize.

This is not an argument for *less* random innovation. Indeed, we need more of it. If we are to understand the healing process or the learning process, there is no substitute for support of undirected basic research by creative people who are permitted to follow where their instincts lead them. Moreover, even in the applied stage, the initial development of new methods and models cannot usefully be systematized. Someone with a new idea about teaching or health service has to work it out on his own, in one place, modifying it and making it operational as he goes along.

But there is a point at which the random innovation model breaks down. If an idea has been reasonably well developed into an operational program and there is some evidence of its success, then what? In the random innovation model, one simply writes up the results and hopes for the best. The good idea may never be noticed. Or it may be too rapidly embraced. One can overestimate the system's resistance to innovation. If it is an attractive, plausible, and not prohibitively expensive idea that does not tread too heavily on the toes of some established professional group, there may even be a rush to try it out. The creators of individually prescribed instruction, for example, were inundated with requests for assistance in implementing their ideas in other school systems even before there were any definitive results on the first project.[2]

---

nation, as well as increasing it, caused output to rise. The same phenomenon has been observed in many social experiments. See David L. Sills (ed.), *International Encyclopedia of the Social Sciences* (Macmillan Company and Free Press, 1968), Vol. 7, p. 241.

2. This learning concept was devised in the Learning Research and Development Center of the University of Pittsburgh.

Systematic Experimentation

But word of mouth and expensive overenthusiasm for an untried concept seem far less reliable than "systematic experimentation" with a new method or model. The innovation should be tried in enough places to establish its capacity to make a difference and the conditions under which it works best. There should be controls to make the new method comparable with the old method or with no action at all. In other words, the conditions of scientific experiments should be realized as nearly as possible.

Systematic experimentation involves enormous problems of organization and execution, for it inherently involves different people in different places—groups of schools or health centers or towns or community organizations—working within a careful overall plan. Furthermore, individual project leaders have to agree to follow the plan and to use common measures of what is done and what is accomplished so that the results can be compared. By contrast, random innovation requires only exhortation plus money and an administrative mechanism for screening out projects that seem to have the greatest chance of success.

The fragmented way in which social services are delivered in the United States makes it relatively easy to engage in random innovation and especially difficult to engage in systematic experimentation. Health service delivery is perhaps the most fragmented of all. Decisions about what to do are made by thousands of individual doctors or by the boards and managers of hundreds of individual clinics, hospitals, and other health facilities. Moreover, even the administrator or the board of directors of a major hospital may regard themselves as having relatively little power to change the way health services are delivered, since they conceive of the hospital as a facility run largely for the convenience of the doctors who practice there. To bring about systematic innovation in health service delivery clearly calls for strong central leadership in the design of a coordinated series of experiments, along with funds or other incentives to reward cooperation. Only a few organizations could manage and finance this kind of a coordinated effort. The most obvious candidate is the federal government.

In education, the situation is a little different and would seem, at first glance, to be more favorable to systematic experimentation. Some states exert a considerable amount of control over local schools. Moreover, large-city school systems are big enough and centralized enough to carry out systematic innovation on a major scale. Indeed, it is surprising that they have not done so. A school superintendent, eager to do a better job, would, it would seem, engage in systematic innovation without any prodding. He would track down the best new ideas in curriculum and approaches and mixes of students and resources, turning for help to literature on experimental projects and results of random innovation in his own and other communities. He would then map out a plan for trying the most promising ideas in a systematic way in his own system, using one approach in several different types of schools and another approach in another set of schools and keeping careful records of the results so that he could extend the productive approaches and phase out the others.

Why does it not happen this way? As William Gorham has pointed out, there are several obvious reasons why systematic innovation is rarely undertaken in school systems:

Because it's "unfair." One must certainly sympathize with the school administrator who is attacked from all sides—by teachers as well as by parents—if he seems to be treating any group differently from any other group. He might very much want to experiment with radical changes in class size, moving to classes of 10 in School A and classes of 40 in School B, and evaluating the results over a period of years. But you can imagine the "unfair" cry he would receive from parents and teachers in School B. He is unlikely to take the risk. Even if the total resources devoted to each child were equal in the two schools, parents in both schools would complain that the method being tried in the other school was better and why weren't their children getting it. Until the necessity for variation and experimentation is well understood by parents and teachers as well as administrators, only the rare administrator will take the risk of offending.

Because it's risky. It is of the essence of experimentation that some experiments don't work. If one is experimenting with physical substances, the cost of failure is time and money. If one is experimenting with children, the cost of failure may be very great. A group of children exposed to a new method of teaching reading may not learn to read. They may feel themselves to be failures because other children exposed to some other method are already reading.

For other reasons. Most school administrators do not have the incentive, the resources, or the know-how to build into their systems a capacity for systematic institutional learning. Their training and experience typically do not motivate or equip them to think in this way. And they really *must* be motivated because they have barriers to overcome—an unsympathetic or complacent community, conflicting demands for resources (for tangible, no-nonsense things like gymnasiums or school band uniforms), staffs or colleagues as difficult to activate as the most conservative elements of the community, and so on.[3]

In other words, systematic experimentation is unlikely to happen spontaneously. An experimental strategy for social reform will have to be devised, organized, and funded by the federal government.

Two attempts at systematic experimentation now under way with federal funds illustrate both some of the potentialities and

3. William Gorham, "Testing and Public Policy" (paper presented at Invitational Conference of the Educational Testing Service, New York, Oct. 28, 1967).

some of the pitfalls of this approach. One is the experiment with a negative income tax. The other is the Follow Through program, a quasi-experimental comparison of various approaches to early childhood education.

Income Maintenance Experiments

Perhaps the best-known example of a social experiment supported by the federal government is the New Jersey Graduated Work Incentive Experiment, funded by the Office of Economic Opportunity. Begun in 1968, this project is an attempt to use the experimental method to answer some of the policy questions that surrounded welfare reform in the mid-1960s.[4]

By the mid-1960s, a fierce debate raged in and out of the government about what was wrong with the welfare system and what could be done about it (see Chapter 2). Some of the differences among the participants in the debate simply reflected differences in values. Those who put a high value on the work ethic were against any solutions that might reduce the incentive for poor people to work. Those who put a high value on human dignity were against any programs that subjected the needy to means tests. Those who put a high value on states' rights or local control were suspicious of federal solutions. Some were emotionally more concerned with the plight of children, some with the problems of the aged poor, some with rural poverty, some with the tragedies of the urban slum.

But besides these differences in values, there were also genuinely different theories about the effect of the present welfare system on human behavior and real ignorance about

4. U.S. Office of Economic Opportunity, "Preliminary Results of the New Jersey Graduated Work Incentive Experiment Conducted by the Office of Economic Opportunity" (Feb. 18, 1970; processed).

how people would respond to a new kind of income maintenance system.

It was clear that the existing welfare system treated families with the same income very differently depending on where they lived and who was in the family. It seemed likely that these differences, besides being inequitable, affected the behavior of the poor, often in perverse ways, and sometimes indistinguishably from more basic factors. For example, a mother with children and inadequate income received greater welfare benefits if she lived in the North than if she lived in the South. This discrepancy created an incentive for families to migrate north; but families migrate for a variety of reasons, and no one knew how many families moved from South to North in response to welfare differentials.

Under the existing welfare system, needy families headed by women generally were eligible for public assistance and those headed by men generally were not, even if they had the same income and the same number of members. A family headed by a man with little or no earning capacity would therefore be better off if the man moved down the street and the woman and children went on welfare. But families break up for a variety of reasons, and no one knew how many were influenced by the incentives built into the welfare laws.

Similarly, it was clear that the existing welfare system provided little incentive to work. Those who were covered by welfare were subject to high marginal tax rates on their earnings. Moreover, a recipient who took a job and got off welfare, but then lost the job, might face a long wait before welfare payments were resumed. Nevertheless, work decisions are complex, and no one knew how many people were deterred from working by the structure of the welfare system.

Concern with the unequal treatment of the poor and the presumed perverse incentives it created stimulated a search for a more general income maintenance system that would aid families and individuals because they were poor, not because they fell into a particular category, and that would extend aid to the working poor without impairing work incentives.

In the effort to resolve these dilemmas, several new approaches to income maintenance were actively discussed, among them variations of a negative income tax.[5] It was clearly an attractive proposal. It was simple in conception. It removed the categories in the welfare system and thus the perverse incentives associated with them. It treated alike all families of the same size and income, whatever the age, sex, or health status of their heads.

But the reason families headed by men had generally been excluded from welfare aid was precisely the fear of impairing their incentive to work. Opponents of a negative income tax claimed that it would induce men in low-income families to quit working or reduce their hours of work. But was it true? Would a negative income tax cause a significant exodus from the labor force? Would the level of the guarantee or the steepness of the marginal tax rate make a difference in working behavior?

The answers to these questions were essential to rational consideration of a negative income tax as an alternative to public assistance. No matter what value was placed on the virtues of work, some basis was needed for estimating the effect of various negative income tax structures on working behavior in order to estimate the cost and effectiveness of the program. If a $3,000 guarantee caused men to drop out of the labor force, then the

5. For a detailed description of the negative income tax, see Chap. 2, esp. pp. 21–22, and note 17. See also James Tobin, Joseph A. Pechman, and Peter M. Mieszkowski, "Is a Negative Income Tax Practical?" *Yale Law Journal*, Vol. 77 (November 1967), pp. 1–27 (Brookings Reprint 142).

program would be more expensive and less effective against poverty than if they continued to seek employment at present welfare rates.

Even rough answers seemed impossible to extract from the available statistics. Since existing programs did not cover most able-bodied men, their statistics could not be used to infer the behavior of men if they were covered. Moreover, even where men were covered (as they were under general assistance in some states), statistics relating payments to earnings did not tell what caused what.

Does individual A receive welfare payments because he has a low earned income, or does he have a low earned income because welfare payments are available to him? Or does causation run in both directions? An experimental approach could resolve this matter, and greatly reduce the area and range of uncertainty.[6]

In view of the importance of the questions and the difficulty of answering them from existing data, the Office of Economic Opportunity decided to experiment with several variants of a negative income tax on a sample of families in several communities and record the results. Interest centered mainly on the administrative feasibility of the program and the effect of alternative guarantees and tax rates on labor force behavior.

Any experiment involving substantial payments to families was bound to be expensive. For example, if payments averaged $1,000 a year per family, an experiment involving a thousand recipient families would cost $1 million a year before any provision was made for costs of administration, data collection, or analysis. Clearly, careful design was crucial if the most important information was to be obtained.

Basic design questions had to be resolved before the experiment could be launched. Should the sample be national or

6. Guy H. Orcutt and Alice G. Orcutt, "Incentive and Disincentive Experimentation for Income Maintenance Policy Purposes," *American Economic Review*, Vol. 58 (September 1968), p. 757.

concentrated in a few communities? Should all kinds of low-income families be represented or only specific types? Which types? How many variants of the guarantee level and tax rate should be tried? Which ones? Should other variations, such as differences in income accounting periods or in reporting procedures, be introduced?

A national sample was appealing because it would presumably yield the best estimates of what might happen if a negative income tax were enacted at the national level. However, if such a sample were relatively small (say, 1,000 to 3,000 families), great variation could be expected during the experimental period in their earnings, and in labor force participation and other behavior, due to variations in local job availability, wage rates, even weather. It would be hard to separate the effects of the negative income tax from the effects of these local factors. Moreover, it would be far more difficult and expensive to maintain contact with a national sample than with a sample concentrated in a few localities.

Including all types of low-income families in the sample was also appealing as a way of anticipating the results of a national negative income tax. But only a relatively small proportion of a varied sample would be working age males, whose work behavior in the face of a negative income tax was of special interest.

Testing a wide variety of combinations of guarantee, marginal tax rate, and other special features of a negative income tax would curtail the risk of omitting some interesting options. But each additional option would require dividing the sample into still smaller groups and reduce the chances that definitive results would show up.

Despite considerable public and congressional criticism, the sample was restricted to low-income families containing an able-bodied man aged 18 to 58, in reflection of the priority accorded to learning as much as possible about the effect of a negative income tax on the work effort of such families.[7] It was also decided that most would be learned from a sample concentrated in the poverty areas of a few neighboring urban communities. Three sites in New Jersey were chosen (Trenton, Paterson-Passaic, and Jersey City). Scranton, Pennsylvania was added, partly to pick up more low-income white families, since the initial sample turned out to be mainly black and Puerto Rican.

Four guarantee levels were chosen, all stated in terms of a percentage of the Social Security Administration's poverty line income. Some families would receive a guarantee of 50 percent of the poverty line; others 75 percent, 100 percent, or 125 percent. Some of the families at each guarantee level were subject to a 50 percent tax on their earnings. Some at the two lowest guarantee levels were subject to a 30 percent rate, providing them greater incentive to increase their earnings, while a group at the middle level paid 70 percent, thus restricting their incentive to earn. Altogether, eight different combinations of guarantee levels and tax rates were established for the experiment. A control sample would be observed, but would receive no payment except a modest inducement to provide information. The whole sample, including the control group, consisted of about 1,350 families.

The experiment was planned to run for three years. First payments were made in Trenton in August 1968, and other cities were added sequentially: Paterson-Passaic in January 1969, Jersey City and Scranton in October 1969.

7. Harold W. Watts describes the program in "Graduated Work Incentives: An Experiment in Negative Taxation," in American Economic Association, *Papers and Proceedings of the Eighty-first Annual Meeting, 1968* (*American Economic Review*, Vol. 59, May 1969), pp. 463–72.

At the time the experiment was conceived, a negative income tax appeared unlikely to receive serious consideration in Congress for several years. But events moved swiftly. In the summer of 1969, President Nixon proposed the Family Assistance Plan (FAP). While not administered through the tax system, the FAP was in essence a negative income tax for families with children, involving a guarantee of approximately 50 percent of the poverty line ($1,600 for a family of four) and a 50 percent marginal tax rate. There was an immediate demand for information on how FAP would work, especially how it would affect the earnings of the previously excluded working poor.

In response to this pressure, OEO hastily put out a short preliminary report for the first year of the New Jersey experiment.[8] The results were notable chiefly for what they did *not* show. The first year's experience revealed no significant differences between negative tax recipients and control families with respect to changes in their earnings. The expectation that a negative tax would induce low-income families to work less was not substantiated. Indeed, the similarity between the experimental and control groups was striking:[9]

Type of family	*Control group*	*Experimental group*
Earnings increased	41%	43%
Earnings did not change	29	28
Earnings decreased	30	29
Total	100	100

8. U.S. Office of Economic Opportunity, "Preliminary Results of the New Jersey Graduated Work Incentive Experiment" (Feb. 18, 1970; processed).

9. These data appear in Harold W. Watts, "Adjusted and Extended Preliminary Results from the Urban Graduated Work Incentive Experiment" (University of Wisconsin, Institute for Research on Poverty, revised June 10, 1970; processed), p. 18. The computation was based on 400 cases in Trenton and Paterson-Passaic after one year of participation. Families were required to move weekly earnings out of an interval $15 wide to show increase or decrease.

Those most intimately connected with the experiment were the quickest to point out that these preliminary results should not be taken too seriously. Harold Watts put it this way:

> In a number of very important respects the evidence from this preliminary and crude analysis of the earliest results is less than ideal. If there were other evidence, approaching the relevance of these data but having fewer problems, it would be highly questionable whether an attempt to interpret and use the New Jersey data currently available should be made. Such is not the case, however, and as a consequence (at risk of being premature) we have tried to be responsibly responsive to a pressing public need for information. That response is simple: No evidence has been found in the urban experiment to support the belief that negative-tax-type income maintenance programs will produce large disincentives and consequent reductions in earnings.[10]

In the meantime, several other experiments were started—in Seattle, Washington, Gary, Indiana, and rural Iowa and North Carolina—to test other types of income maintenance systems, coordination of income maintenance with other public programs, notably manpower and social services, and the behavior of other kinds of families, especially those headed by a female, and the rural poor.[11] Out of these efforts should come a base of information for improving our income maintenance system firmer than any we have had before.

There are, of course, some questions to answer before extrapolating from any income maintenance experiment to a national

10. *Ibid.*, p. 40.

11. D. Lee Bawden, "Income Maintenance and the Rural Poor: An Experimental Approach," *American Journal of Agricultural Economics*, Vol. 52 (August 1970), pp. 438–41; Robert Spiegelman, "Prospectus: Seattle Income Maintenance Experiment," Proposal #MU69-359, prepared for the State of Washington Department of Public Assistance and U.S. Department of Health, Education, and Welfare (Stanford Research Institute, September 1969; mimeo.); Terence F. Kelly and Leslie Singer, "The Gary Income Maintenance Experiment: Plans and Progress," a version of which will appear in American Economic Association, *Papers and Proceedings of the Eighty-third Annual Meeting, 1970* (*American Economic Review*, Vol. 61, May 1971).

income maintenance system. Since participants in the experiment know their good fortune is temporary, will they behave differently from the way they would behave if the change were permanent? Since only a few people have been singled out for the experiment, will they behave differently from the way they would behave if all their neighbors were also participants? Since participants in the experiment know they are being observed, will they keep more honest records than they would if they were not observed? Will they buy different things? We do not have enough experience with social experiments to answer these questions. In a sense these experiments test not only substantive issues but the validity of social experimentation itself.

The Follow Through Program

The Follow Through program is another example of a current attempt to use federal funds to learn how to produce services effectively—in this case, services for young children. Follow Through is a quasi-experiment, with a statistical design far less sophisticated than that of the New Jersey income maintenance experiment. There was evidence that children could move ahead rapidly in a good preschool program, but that when they were dumped back into the same dismal slum school the gains were lost. The objective of Follow Through was to determine whether the gains achieved through Headstart could be maintained through special programs in the early years of elementary school.

Follow Through was originally planned as a fairly large program, to be budgeted at about $100 million for the first full year and to receive larger sums thereafter. The program was administratively anomalous, however; it appeared in the budget of the Office of Economic Opportunity but was to be managed by the Office of Education, an arrangement that made no one clearly responsible for assuring program funding. OEO was reluctant to fight hard for a program it did not manage; the Office of Education had no mechanism to promote a program that did not appear in its budget. Perhaps because of this anomaly, Follow Through was funded at a very low level—under $15 million for the first year.

The low funding was probably a blessing in disguise. Since the sum provided was clearly not sufficient to finance a national service program for children "graduating" from Headstart, it was decided to use what was available to try out in a systematic way several approaches to early childhood education and evaluate their effectiveness.

There was no lack of ideas about how to reach small children. Some radically new approaches had been developed by scholars and tried out in laboratory schools with considerable success, but there was little evidence about how they would work in a regular school environment. The first steps in Follow Through were to identify some of these approaches, to invite the developers to describe what they were doing, and to seek their guidance for communities that put their methods into practice. The response was excellent. A number of scholars committed themselves to be "sponsors"—that is, to undertake the major administrative assignment of helping communities organize and implement Follow Through.

The approaches were extremely varied. The Becker-Engelmann program, developed at the University of Illinois, emphasized intensive work with small groups of children on the cognitive skills that deprived children often lack—verbal expression, reading, mathematical skills. The methods involve rapid-fire questioning of students by instructors with rewards in the form of praise and stars for right answers. It is a highly disciplined approach and has been described as an intellectual "pressure cooker." By contrast, the program of the Bank Street College of Education in New York takes a far more relaxed approach, minimizing drill and emphasizing learning by doing, such as caring for pets. The Bank Street approach relies on organizing the environment of the school so the child can learn in his own style and at his own pace.

Another approach, developed by Bushell at the University of Kansas, among others, emphasizes the concept of reinforcement of learning through rewards for appropriate behavior. Children earn tokens that are exchangeable for privileges and food. A child who performs well can even buy a chance to be naughty—perhaps to make a loud noise, but not to hit another child over the head! Still other approaches emphasize the training of parents and their use in the school.[12]

The Follow Through plan was to invite communities to try one or another of these approaches and to assess and compare the results over a period of years. When the strategy was first proposed, many of the old hands in the Office of Education predicted political disaster. They were afraid the office would be accused of federal control, of telling school people what to do. Some anticipated an outcry from the chief state school officers and congressional antagonism to the program. Perhaps the developers of Follow Through were clever; perhaps they were just lucky. The antagonism never came.

The states were invited to nominate communities that had an interest in undertaking a Follow Through project and seemed likely to be able to do it successfully. Representatives of these communities were invited to a series of meetings at which the different approaches were described and explained, and the

12. Robert L. Egbert, "Descriptions of Follow Through Approaches" (U.S. Office of Education, internal memorandum, March 14, 1969).

federal government's promise of money and the technical assistance of one of the sponsors was held out in exchange for agreement to carry out one of the approaches and cooperate in its evaluation. Although some approaches were far more popular than others, the response was generally enthusiastic. Projects and sponsors were added, and Stanford Research Institute undertook to evaluate the program.

Since Follow Through was not a scientifically designed experiment, there is reason to question whether valid conclusions can be drawn from it about the relative effectiveness of the various approaches.[13] The participating communities were not randomly selected, nor were the approaches matched with communities in a random manner. In each community classrooms not participating in Follow Through, but similar to those that were, were designated as control groups, but again not randomly. Except in a few cases, only a relatively small number of communities tried a given approach. A considerable amount of variation is likely to show up within any group of projects utilizing the "same" approach, due to differences in the communities and in the way the approach was implemented. Furthermore, some sponsors are better administrators than others and it is not always easy to get a community to carry out what the sponsor originally intended. In the end, differences within approaches may swamp any attempt to make comparisons across approaches. In any case, there are not enough projects of any one type to support definitive statements about what works best with different kinds of population.

Moreover, conceptual problems arise in defining goals and measures of success even for individual projects. There is

13. David K. Cohen, "Politics and Research: Evaluation of Social Action Programs in Education," *Review of Educational Research*, Vol. 40 (April 1970), pp. 213–38.

greater difficulty in comparing approaches in part because they have different goals. One expects children in a program that places heavy emphasis on reading to score well on reading tests. But children in a program that emphasizes self-reliance or curiosity or verbal expressiveness might have developed greatly in these respects and still not score well on a reading test. The problem is to develop suitable sets of measuring instruments that reflect progress in different dimensions and that can be applied across projects of differing emphasis.

As long as no one is seeking a definitive "best" approach, the problem of multiple objectives and multiple success measures does not seem insurmountable. Approaches can be evaluated against standards appropriate to each, and the results displayed. It is not necessary to weight the various measures. Communities seeking information about success of these approaches can choose those that fit in well with their own objectives. The main danger is that noncognitive characteristics like self-reliance and intellectual curiosity cannot be adequately measured and so will tend to get lost.

Despite its shortcomings in experimental design, Follow Through is significant as the first major attempt on the part of the federal government to try out different educational approaches in a reasonably systematic way.

Other Education Experiments

Whether systematic experimentation is to become a main theme of federal education efforts or a minor sidelight remains unclear. Two kinds of experiments are currently of special interest, performance contracting and voucher systems.

Performance contracting is an attempt to harness the profit motive to improvement of the effectiveness of teaching.[14] The

14. For a discussion of voucher systems, see Chap. 6.

notion is that regular public school teachers may lack incentives to make a maximum effort to impart intellectual skills, especially to hard-to-teach children. They may be too inflexible to try new methods, or inhibited by past failures or the conviction that children from impoverished or minority families are doomed to failure no matter what the teacher does. Not paid or promoted on the basis of how much the children learn, individual teachers or administrators may not have much stake in the children's success. Performance contracting would break this alleged cycle of self-fulfilling expectations by allowing school systems to contract with private firms that would undertake to increase the measured performance of children in, say, reading or mathematics, and that would be paid according to their success.

Federal attempts to try out performance contracting got off to an inauspicious start. The Office of Education funded a project in Texarkana aimed at improving reading and mathematics skills, in which a group of children were released from school for three hours a day of instruction by a private firm. The firm was to be paid a fee for each child whose tested performance rose a whole grade level within a specified time period, and a penalty was to be imposed if the child's performance had slipped back when he was retested six months later.

The first results in Texarkana were encouraging. The children taught by the contractor apparently made dramatic gains, far greater than had been expected. But then evidence came to light suggesting that the contractor had influenced the results by giving the children a chance to practice on the test questions during their regular instruction. The project was abruptly terminated.[15]

Despite this unpromising beginning, the Office of Economic Opportunity considers the concept of performance contracting

15. *New York Times*, May 15 and 24, 1970, and *Washington Post*, Sept. 20, 1970.

worth pursuing if safeguards are built in to avoid repetition of the Texarkana experience, and has moved ahead with a series of experiments.[16]

The Pros and Cons of an Experimental Strategy

The argument for systematic experimentation is straightforward: Information necessary to improve the effectiveness of social services is impossible to obtain any other way. In the absence of deliberate experimentation, new methods of delivering social services are implemented only sporadically or in combination with other factors that influence their apparent success. New methods must be tried out systematically under a variety of conditions if their effectiveness is to be evaluated accurately. Similarly, it is often impossible to predict how individuals will behave in the face of a novel pattern of incentives. To start up a major national program that affected incentives to work or to increase productivity, and to discover that the incentives did not operate in the expected direction, might prove very costly. Common sense suggests trying the program on a small scale to gain advance knowledge about effects on incentives.

This general argument implies that the federal government should undertake the design and evaluation of social experiments as a major task in the 1970s. These need not be confined to one area of social action. One set could be aimed at evaluating approaches to teaching at all levels—new kinds of curricula, teacher training methods, and recruitment policies; mixes of teachers with various levels of training; various patterns of parent participation. Another might assess day care in large and small centers and family arrangements. Store front or neighborhood centers, hospital-based care, and mixes of variously

16. *Washington Post*, July 15, 1970.

skilled personnel could be tried out as alternative arrangements for delivering medical services. Other sets of experiments might explore the responses of individuals and institutions to different types of incentives—capitation versus fee-for-service payments in medicine, voucher systems versus tax support of education. The list could go on and on.

But many thoughtful people have doubts about an experimental strategy. They have qualms about the ethics of experimenting with people, doubts about the political feasibility of experimentation, and technical reservations about the validity of experimental results in the social action area. The remainder of this chapter will examine some of these objections and their validity.

First, there is the ethical question: Does society have the right to take risks with the lives and well-being of individuals in the name of experimentation? In the medical and pharmacological area, where experiments can result in death and permanent injury, this problem is obvious and serious. It has generated much discussion and many attempts to formulate codes of ethics.[17] In the social action area, where experiments rarely involve death or physical damage, the problem seems less serious, but is perhaps only less obvious. Experiments with new ways of organizing or paying for health services, for example, could result in preventable deaths or illness. New kinds of teaching methods or early child care might do psychological damage of a more subtle sort. Tremendous care has to be taken to anticipate and avoid such risks and to weigh them against the risks of existing practices. People die from lack of medical care and children suffer from current school methods. The risks of change have to be weighed against the risks of no change.

17. For a brief discussion, see Bernard Barber, "Experimenting with Humans," *Public Interest*, No. 6 (Winter 1967), pp. 91–102.

Including individuals in a social experiment probably presents less difficult ethical problems than excluding them. In general, social experiments are undertaken to determine whether an apparently promising new approach is indeed superior to existing practice and how it works under various conditions. To make these judgments, it is necessary to give the new service to some people and to deny it to others. But is this fair, and how are the favored few to be chosen?

As a former general counsel of HEW has pointed out, the courts are only beginning to come to grips with the problems raised by unequal distribution of publicly provided services. They have yet to give any real guidance on the equity of inequalities deliberately created for experimental purposes. They have not faced up to questions like these:

> Is it right, for example, to deny service to a man who lives on the wrong side of the street merely because his inclusion might obscure the statistical base for evaluation of the project? And what are we to say of the use of control groups, chosen to be as similar to the aided groups as possible but denied benefits in order to serve as a base for comparison?[18]

Whichever way the courts move, organizers of experiments clearly have a public responsibility to be sure that the knowledge to be gained will justify the denial of service.

Legal and moral issues aside, it will be politically difficult to provide services to some people and not others in the name of experimentation. Indeed, cutting back on an existing service generally thought to be beneficial is likely to be politically impossible. Failure to extend a new service to everybody at once may be more easily tolerated. If the service is costly or involves

18. Alanson W. Willcox, "Public Services under a Government of Laws," in U.S. Department of Health, Education, and Welfare, "What's Going On In HEW?" *HEW Forum Papers*, 1967–1968, p. 106.

some limited resource, such as people with special skills, there may be little resentment against an experiment. As Campbell has pointed out, the fact that the Salk vaccine was in short supply the first year after its development made possible a large-scale experiment with its effectiveness.[19] Since there was not enough vaccine for everyone, it did not seem immoral to pick certain children to receive it and give others placebo injections. Had there been enough to go around, it would have seemed unconscionable to withhold it from some children, even if its effectiveness had not been fully documented.

Negative income tax payments, while perhaps not lifesaving, must seem nearly so to poor families. If budgetary resources had been available to extend aid to all needy families in 1968, the New Jersey experiment would have seemed grossly inequitable. At the time the project was designed, however, prospects for immediate enactment of a universal income maintenance system were dim. This fact made it possible to try several variations of a negative income tax on a sample of families without much public concern over the ethics of helping some but not others.

Even when resources are scarce, however, concern for fairness may inhibit good experimental design. A valid experiment requires that individuals be assigned to treatment or control groups by a random selection process. Chance must enter. A government official may find it far more difficult to explain to the public that he is allocating a scarce resource on the basis of chance than to defend some other selection criterion such as need or merit or "first come, first served." But if such criteria are used, those not selected cannot be regarded as a control group; their behavior cannot validly be compared with that of

19. Donald T. Campbell, "Reforms as Experiments," *American Psychologist*, Vol. 24 (April 1969), p. 419.

the treatment group to establish the effectiveness of the treatment, because the two groups may differ in important ways.

In the past, many opportunities for experimentation have slipped away because no one had the courage or the foresight to insist on random selection. For example, several evaluations of Neighborhood Youth Corps (NYC) projects indicated that trainees scored higher on a number of success measures than similar young people who were not in NYC.[20] The comparisons were of dubious value, however, because of the possibility that young people who volunteer and are selected for NYC are more highly motivated and smarter than students with the same demographic characteristics who are not in NYC. Since there were far more volunteers than could be served by the program, it would have been possible to select NYC trainees by a random process and to compare them with a control group. But the program was not designed with a view to learning about its effectiveness.

Another reservation about the desirability of social experimentation concerns the honesty with which experimental results will be reported. No one likes to fail. Rightly or wrongly, the administrator of a successful experimental project will receive more acclaim and greater opportunities for advancement than the administrator of an unsuccessful project. Under these circumstances will there not be a temptation to cheat a bit—to choose the most favorable measuring instruments, to "lose" the records of children who fail or patients who die, to coach participants on what to say to the evaluator or how to beat the test?

The Texarkana incident provides evidence, if any were needed,

20. For example, Gerald G. Somers and Ernst W. Stromsdorfer, "A Cost-Effectiveness Study of the In-School and Summer Neighborhood Youth Corps" (University of Wisconsin, Industrial Relations Research Institute, July 1970).

that concern about the honesty of social experiments is legitimate. Nevertheless, safeguards are available. Clearly, the manager of an experimental program should not also be the evaluator. He should not choose or administer tests or other measuring instruments and he should be under surveillance designed to catch more subtle forms of conscious or unconscious cheating. Although no safeguard is perfect, independent evaluation and vigorous supervision should avoid serious abuses.

Even if experiments are honestly conducted, one might fear political interference in reporting of results. Will government officials be willing to release results that show failure of a program to which an agency is already committed? Or, where the experimental results are mixed, might there not be a tendency to emphasize and publicize the positive results while deemphasizing, if not actually suppressing, the negative ones?

The eagerness of the government to produce results from the New Jersey experiment that would bolster the case for the family assistance plan dramatizes the dangers of political use of experimental results. It happened that the preliminary data from the experiment supported the administration's contention that supplementing the income of the working poor would not lead to an exodus from the labor force. If they had come out the other way, the early results might have been regarded (in this case rightly) as "too preliminary" for publication.

While the possibility of less than totally honest use of experimental results exists, it does not seem a valid reason to forgo the potential benefits of an experimental strategy. A major effort to find better ways of delivering social services by experimental means necessitates the development of a code of ethics. This does not seem impossible. Most physical scientists have a strong moral commitment to seeking "truth" and to honest reporting of experimental results. While some may cheat, one suspects there is very little of this, both because of the moral commitment and because no scientist could afford to be caught doctoring data or suppressing unfavorable results. Experiments can be replicated, so the danger of being caught is great. One would hope that, as social experimentation becomes more widespread, high standards of ethics would be maintained and that public officials would respect them and find it impolitic to be caught transgressing them.

But even if social experiments can be honestly run and fairly reported, the validity of this kind of strategy in the social action area is vulnerable to technical problems. (1) Is it possible to replicate social experiments, to do the "same" thing enough times to generalize about it? (2) Are the results of an experiment compromised by the fact that it is an experiment and the subjects know it? (3) Is evidence from small-scale trials of a policy a valid basis for predicting what would happen if the whole country were subject to it? (4) Does the length of time required to assess the ultimate results of a social change preclude the use of experiments for social policy formulation?

An important element in physical experiments is the exact specification of what is to be done in the experiment and control of all the factors that might affect the results. If some factors cannot be controlled, the experiment must be repeated a sufficient number of times to average out the effects of the uncontrolled elements. It is important that the same specifications be followed each time the experiment is repeated.

Imagine, for example, an experiment to determine which of two types of seed corn produces the greatest yield. Since the weather or other environmental conditions that may affect the results are not susceptible to control, it is necessary to try the two types quite a few times—and in exactly the same way each time. The plants must always be the same distance apart, cultivated with the same frequency, and fed the same fertilizer. Otherwise the experiment is ruined.

In the social action area, it is much more difficult to replicate an experiment exactly. Even in an income maintenance experiment, in which payment schedules and eligibility rules have been exactly specified, unexpected problems are likely to arise. It may be necessary to decide without delay what to say to a recipient who seeks help in filling out forms or how to treat a deviant family living arrangement. If such decisions are not made the same way in successive trials, the validity of the conclusions may be affected.

In experiments with education or health services, the scope for variation is much greater. In comparing two methods of reading instruction, for example, no one can tell the teacher exactly what to do in every situation that may arise in the classroom. Indeed, to do this would be to turn the teacher into an unthinking automaton and probably to doom the experiment. Teachers must be allowed some scope for adapting the method to the needs of their students. The most creative teachers are likely to alter the method substantially as they go along, rejecting elements that seem not to be working and substituting others.

Hence, one must expect and allow some variation from one classroom to the next in the application of new techniques. But not too much. If there is wide variation in what is done in classrooms supposedly following method A or method B, it will overwhelm any differences that exist between the two, thus jeopardizing the experiment.

There is probably no way to overcome this problem. No good teacher or doctor or social worker will participate wholeheartedly in an experiment in which his every word is programmed and his freedom to adapt methods to circumstances is completely circumscribed. More experience with the concept of experimentation and education on the importance of adhering to the design would reduce these deviations. Nevertheless, it would not be desirable to reduce them to zero. The likelihood of differences has to be allowed for in the design of the experiment itself. It will take a larger number of trials of two methods to detect a significant difference between them if there is substantial variation within the two sets. Proper interpretation of the results also calls for careful recording of exactly what was done in each instance.

Another difficulty with social experiments is that, in general, the people who participate know they are part of an experiment. They may behave differently because they know they are being watched. One might wonder, for example, whether the spending patterns or even the working hours of the participants in the New Jersey experiment are influenced by the knowledge that they have to report what they do.

As mentioned earlier, there is also some reason to believe that individuals will perform at a higher level when something—anything—new and different is happening to them. This phenomenon, sometimes known as the Hawthorne effect,[21] may cause a new method to appear more successful than the old when it is only the newness, not the method itself, that brings about the improvement. While we should be careful not to be misled by the Hawthorne effect, its existence can be an asset to social action. If change itself can be shown to be beneficial, then we can work to institutionalize change.

Another problem with social experiments is that the behavior of participants in a small-scale experiment may differ from that in a large-scale experiment or a national program. People are influenced by what they see their neighbors and associates doing.

21. See note 1, pp. 89–90.

This community interaction effect clearly is one of the problems of the New Jersey income maintenance experiment. If only one family on the block receives payments, its members may continue to behave much as their neighbors do. They probably continue to go to work because their neighbors go to work and to follow the spending patterns of the community around them. If the whole community were receiving the same level of negative tax payments, what was considered normal behavior might gradually shift.

One way to mitigate this problem is to run social experiments in neighborhoods or whole communities at once. This is expensive, however, and there are compensating disadvantages. Special local conditions, such as a high unemployment rate, may have a strong influence on the outcome of the experiment run only in one or two communities.

Finally, social experiments may simply take too much time. Many of the really interesting effects of social action show up only after a period of years. An experiment in preschool education, for example, may uncover a method of significantly increasing the capacity of children to learn to read in first grade. But reading in first grade is not an end in itself; it is a means to higher performance in later years of school and to higher levels of intellectual skills as an adult. Similarly, the importance of an income maintenance program may lie not in the immediate effect on the behavior of the adults in the family, but in the school performance, attitudes, and future of the children. The significant results of the experiment may not be known in time to affect the policy decision at issue.

Here the crucial problem is to decide whether an incomplete experiment is preferable to no experiment at all. If there seems to be a reasonable probability that the initial results of the experiment will give some clues to the longer-term effects, then the experiment may lead to substantially better policy decisions even if the ultimate effects cannot be known for some time. The New Jersey experiment was designed primarily to find out whether people who receive negative tax payments reduce their work hours significantly. This knowledge is basic to an assessment of the costs of a negative income tax, even if the longer-term benefits (or costs) cannot be determined experimentally in time to affect the decision.

This objection, however, suggests another political hazard of a social experimentation strategy: Experiments may become substitutes for action or excuses for inaction. Since the full effects of any social action are impossible to predict, experimentation will give the foot-draggers an excuse: "We can't act now, we must wait for the results of the experiments." Instead of becoming a tool for improving the effectiveness of social action, experimentation could become an excuse for devoting fewer resources to it.

The danger is real. Nevertheless, to forgo needed social experiments on the grounds that they might delay social change seems foolish. Action and experimentation are not mutually exclusive. A community or a nation that wants to act can act and experiment at the same time. In the case of Headstart, for example, hindsight suggests that a large-scale, immediate program and a smaller-scale program of experiments to discover how to help preschool children effectively could have existed side by side. Funds allocated to systematic experimentation not only would not have delayed the action program; they might very well have made it more effective in the end.

On balance, I believe the advantages of social experimentation far outweigh the disadvantages, and that the federal government should follow a systematic experimentation strategy in seeking to improve the effectiveness of social action programs. The process will not be easy or quick or cheap. Nor can one look forward to an end to it. It would be a mistake to adopt systematic experimentation in the hope that it would "tell us what works." The phrase suggests that there is some all-time optimum way of organizing social services and that we are going to find it and then quit. Clearly the world is not like this. What works for one place or one generation will not work for another. The process of developing new methods, trying them out, modifying them, trying again, will have to be continuous. But unless we begin searching for improvements and experimenting with them in a systematic way, it is hard to see how we will make much progress in increasing the effectiveness of our social services.

6 Accountability: What Does It Mean?

The two preceding chapters dealt with three strategies for finding more effective methods of producing education, health, and other social services: (1) analysis of the "natural experiment," (2) random innovation, and (3) systematic experimentation. The major conclusion was that all three strategies should be pursued with increased energy and greater methodological sophistication.

Analysis of the natural experiment has not yet turned up many clues to more effective ways of producing social services. But with time and more refined techniques, there is hope that it will. As a necessary first step to more effective services, all kinds of people should be encouraged to try out new ways of delivering services. But random innovation does not yield knowledge of what works best for whom or under what conditions. This requires systematic experimentation—with new curricula, new training techniques, new ways of delivering medical care. As the last chapter indicated, I believe systematic experimentation must be an important federal activity if we are to achieve breakthroughs in social service delivery.

But finding more effective methods is not enough. How do we know they will be used? What incentives are built into our social service systems to encourage effectiveness?

As the public sector of our economy grows larger, the problem of building incentives to effective performance into public programs becomes more and more crucial. As Schultze pointed out in his Gaither lectures, federal programs have often failed to reach their objectives because no thought was given to incentives:

> The failure of performance stems from two related causes. The first of these is "negative failure"—the failure to take account of private incentives that run counter to program objectives, and to provide for appropriate modifications in existing rewards and penalties that thwart social objectives. . . .

The second cause is "positive failure"—the failure to build into federal programs a positive set of incentives to channel the activities of decentralized administrators and program operators toward the program objectives.[1]

In the social action area, the problem is both especially acute and especially difficult. Present arrangements for delivering social services provide few rewards for those who produce better education or health service, few penalties for those who fail to produce. School systems are big bureaucracies serving a largely captive clientele. Students and their parents have little freedom to move from one school to another in search of a "better" education, and hardly any information by which to judge the effectiveness of schools. Teachers, principals, and superintendents are rarely rewarded or promoted on the basis of the educational results they achieve. State and federal financing is not designed to reward effective performance of schools or school systems.

The health system *looks* different. There are far more small units—hospitals, clinics, and doctors in private practice—and the consumer seems to have choice. But in fact he has neither the time, the resources, nor the knowledge on which to base an intelligent choice. Moreover, in health as in education, payment mechanisms fail to reward efficiency or effectiveness. On the contrary, the present health insurance systems, both public and private, operate to encourage overuse of hospitals—the most expensive health facilities—and fail to encourage the development and use of less costly alternatives.

The diagnosis is clear, but what is the prescription? It is easy to talk loosely about holding producers of education and health services "accountable" for their performance to those who consume the services and to those who pay for them. But it is hard

1. Charles L. Schultze, *The Politics and Economics of Public Spending* (Brookings Institution, 1968), pp. 104–05.

to design a workable set of measures of performance, to decide exactly what accounts are to be rendered to whom and how rewards and penalties are to be meted out.

This chapter will deal with three models for improving the effectiveness with which social services are produced. One is decentralization—breaking up central administrative units, like school systems or federal programs, into more manageable units. The second is community control—a step beyond decentralization in which control of schools or other services is turned over to the community being served, in the hope of making producers more responsive to consumers. The last is the "market model," perhaps the most extreme form of decentralization. If the market model were applied to education, for one example, students would be given a choice among publicly, or privately, operated schools. Reliance would be placed on competition among schools to spur more effective educational methods.

Decentralization, community control, and a market system have all been advertised as panaceas. One or the other, it has been suggested, would solve the problem of incentives, even eliminate the need for central government efforts to discover and encourage more effective methods. The message of this chapter is that, while all three models hold out some promise, none is a cure-all. In particular, the success of all three depends on two conditions: (1) the development and use of better measures of the effectiveness of social services; and (2) vigorous and systematic attempts to find and test more effective methods and to publicize the results.

Decentralization

Decentralization of decision making, at least down to the state or city level, has always been popular with conservatives—those who generally oppose expansion of the public sector and changes in methods of delivering services. Rejecting "frills" and "new-fangled" devices in the school and clinging to fee-for-service medicine and traditional health facilities, these groups have always fought for local control and less interference from Washington or the state capital. But the remarkable political development of the last several years has been the conversion of liberals—those who favor more public services and newer methods—to the cause of decentralization. Why the switch?

One element is a new realism about the capacity of a central government to manage social action programs effectively. There was a time when those who believed in broader public commitment to social action pinned their hopes on centralization. Finding themselves stymied by conservatism, rigidity, and lack of resources at the local level, they turned to state government. Finding the states unresponsive, they turned—especially after 1933—to the federal government.

But the last several years have seen a marked shift in the attitude of liberals toward the federal role. I am not referring to the carping criticism of academics or of the party out of power about the "bungling and inefficiency" of federal executives. Those who happen not to be running the government at the moment have always griped, with more or less justification, about the ineptitude of those who were. Rather, I am talking about the change of attitude that occurred during the 1960s among those who helped design federal social action programs and tried to make them work.

I, for one, once thought that the effectiveness of a program like Headstart or Title I of the Elementary and Secondary Education Act could be increased by tighter management from Washington. Something was known about "good practices," or effective ways of reaching poor children; more could be learned and transmitted to the local level through federal guidelines and regulations and technical assistance. As knowledge accumulated, the guidelines could be tightened up, and programs would become more effective.

This view now seems to me naïve and unrealistic. The country is too big and too diverse, and social action is too complicated. There are over 25,000 school districts, and their needs, problems and capacities differ drastically. Universal rules are likely to do more harm than good. Nor, given the numbers of people involved, is it possible simply to rely on the judgment or discretion of federal representatives in the field.

Robert Levine, former planning officer for the Office of Economic Opportunity, has given a good description of the new realism:

> By and large, those programs which have stressed detailed planning and detailed administration have either not worked, or have worked only on a scale which was very small compared to the size of the problem. . . . The detailed administrative approach does not work for clear enough reasons—which start with the impossibility of writing detailed rules to fit every case, and end with the lack of highly trained people to administer every case, assuming even that an administrative solution is possible. . . . The setbacks of the War on Poverty arise, in part, from the difficulties of applying a specific and administered program to more than 30 million poor individuals. . . . What we might be able to achieve is a long-run redesign of the Poverty Program to reduce the amount of detailed administration, and to provide more incentives for individuals to develop their own programs.[2]

The new realists are not ready to give up on the federal government and turn social action programs back to state and local governments. One cogent reason is the inequality of state and local resources. The states with the greatest per capita

2. Robert A. Levine, "Rethinking Our Social Strategies," *Public Interest*, No. 10 (Winter 1968), pp. 88, 89, 91, 92.

needs for education, health, income maintenance, and other social action programs also have the lowest per capita resources. Even within states, resources are frequently concentrated where the problems are least acute. Central cities find themselves facing mounting needs for public services and falling tax bases, while the resources of the suburbs are far greater in relation to need. The intervention of the federal government is required to channel resources to areas of need, a task that, fortunately, it is well equipped to handle.

Two activities that the federal bureaucracy carries out with great efficiency are collecting taxes and writing checks. For all its faults, the federal tax system is certainly among the most equitable and efficient in the world. Federal taxation falls largely on income, and hence is more progressive than state and local taxation, which falls largely on property and sales and thus on the poor. The progressivity of the federal system, moreover, makes it more responsive to economic growth than state and local systems. Unless rates are lowered, federal revenues tend to rise faster than the national income—a fortunate fact in an age when the demand for public services is rising more rapidly than income. Finally, income taxes are easier and cheaper to collect than are property and sales taxes, and are far less subject to the whims and errors of individual assessors.

The efficiency with which the federal government collects money is matched by the efficiency with which it disburses it. The social security system, the Veterans Administration, and other federal agencies charged with making payments directly to individuals discharge their responsibilities apparently with a minimum of difficulty and confusion.

Since the federal government is good at collecting and handing out money, but inept at administering service programs, then it might make sense to restrict its role in social action mainly to tax collection and check writing and leave the detailed administration of social action programs to smaller units. This view implies cutting out categorical grants-in-aid with detailed guidelines and expenditure controls. Instead, the major federal domestic activity would be the distribution of funds to individuals and governments on the basis of need and other criteria. The mechanism for distributing funds to individuals would be social security, family assistance, or other forms of income maintenance. Lower levels of government would receive funds through revenue sharing or bloc grants for general purposes like education. The last two federal budgets, with their emphasis on income maintenance and revenue sharing, appear to be moving the federal government in this direction.

But a deep-seated fear that the money will be misused and misdirected has always made the liberals—and, indeed, most of the Congress—leary of turning over federal tax money to lower levels of government without strict guidelines. How does the federal taxpayer know that his funds will be spent efficiently and effectively? While it may be easier in principle to manage programs at the state or local level than to deal with the vastness and diversity of the nation as a whole, in practice state and local governments have hardly been models of efficiency, effectiveness, or even honesty. Moreover, not sharing national objectives, state and local governments may underfund such programs as higher education or pollution control whose benefits are likely to spill over into other jurisdictions. They may be dominated by a small, local power elite. The federal taxpayer clearly has grounds for insisting that lower levels of government be held "accountable" to the federal government for the uses they make of federal funds.

But stating the accountability in terms of inputs—through detailed guidelines and controls on objects of expenditure—

spawns red tape and rigidity without introducing incentives to more outputs. Hence a new approach is in order: State the accountability in terms of outputs, and reward those who produce more efficiently. Free to vary the way they spend the money as long as they accomplish specified results, recipients of federal grants could be rewarded for producing beyond expectations. This procedure would liberate them from the strait-jacket of input controls and promote vigorous and imaginative attempts to improve results, just as in large corporations plant managers are free to vary production methods, but are rewarded and promoted according to sales and profits.

This reasoning applies, of course, not just to federal relations with state and local governments, but to the broader question of productivity incentives in any large bureaucratic enterprise. Even in programs run by the federal government itself, productivity could be increased by allowing individual project managers—federal hospital administrators or training center heads, for example—more freedom of action and more incentive to achievement. Similar reasoning has led many to advocate decentralization of big-city school districts into semi-autonomous units that would be freed from rigid restrictions on curriculum, teaching methods, or mix of resources, and rewarded for producing better educational results.

The idea of accountability certainly sounds simple and sensible and right. Implementing it is harder. Most social action programs have vague and diverse goals, and agreement on how to measure their success is far from complete. Little serious work has been done to develop the objective measures of performance that are needed to implement this concept of accountability.

One might think, for example, that performance measures could be readily devised for manpower training programs. Their goals—to increase the employability and improve the earning capacity of trainees—are not esoteric. Success can be measured in rates at which trainees are placed in jobs, and retain and advance in them, and in differentials between what they earn and what they would have earned without the training. Good management practice suggests considerable freedom for project managers in designing programs suited to local conditions and to the needs of their trainees, and in rating the projects according to these objective criteria.

But even in manpower training, performance measures are difficult to devise. One problem is dealing with several different, albeit related, objectives. If manpower training projects were judged only on their success in job placement, there would be pressure to place trainees in jobs as quickly as possible regardless of the wage level, suitability, stability, or possibilities of advancement in the employment. The result would be a lot of placements in low-level, dead-end jobs, and little contribution to productivity. On the other hand, if increases in earnings were the sole criterion, programs would probably concentrate on people whose skills were already well developed and on younger workers with a longer earning life ahead of them. Some kind of weighted average of several success measures (job placements, earnings increases, retention rates, and so forth) would avoid distortion of the objectives of the program.

In addition, success measures have to be related to the difficulty of the problem. It is more difficult to find jobs for trainees if the local unemployment rate is high. It is harder and more expensive to train and place older people than younger people, poorly educated people than better educated people. Completion rates and wage rates are likely to be higher for men than for women. Such variations have to be taken into consideration in rating the performance of a project, both out of fairness to the project manager and to prevent "creaming," the tendency to enroll only those who will be easy to train and place. A rating system meeting these criteria was developed for assessing the effectiveness of projects under the Work Experience and Training Program in HEW, but was not used.[3]

Objectives are less easy to define in other social action areas than in manpower training, and work on performance measures is in an even more primitive stage. Incorporating performance incentives into education programs is intriguing, but a workable mechanism will be hard to design. A simple formula, based, for example, on high reading scores, might do more harm than good, by rewarding districts with easy-to-teach children, or by encouraging instruction solely for results on a specific test and overemphasis on reading at the expense of other educational values. The trick will be to develop measures that reflect the educational achievement of the schools without distorting programs in counterproductive directions.

Unless the effort is made to develop performance measures and use them as incentives, it is hard to see how decentralization by itself will lead to greater effectiveness. Without incentives to produce, small units are not obviously better than large ones.

Moreover, there are some governmental functions that would almost certainly suffer from decentralization. One is research and development. Small units are unlikely to invest in such a risky activity when most of the benefit is likely to go to other units. Moreover, for any hope of success, some problems demand a critical mass of talent and resources that only the federal government can mobilize. The atomic and hydrogen bombs, the lunar landings, and some of the federally sponsored break-

3. Worth Bateman, "Assessing Program Effectiveness," U.S. Department of Health, Education, and Welfare, *Welfare in Review*, Vol. 6 (January/February 1968), pp. 1–10.

throughs in biomedical research are ample evidence of the federal ability to put the requisite resources to work on a scientific problem. Breakthroughs in social service delivery seem likely to require similar concentrations of effort.

Community Control

The push for decentralization comes at least partly from frustration at the top bred from the realization that very large units cannot manage social action programs effectively. The push for community control comes from frustration at the bottom. The supposed beneficiaries of social action programs, especially the poor and the black, feel themselves objects rather than participants in the process. The demand for community control, especially in the ghetto, reflects the feeling that schools and hospitals and welfare centers are alien institutions run by hostile members of another culture unable to understand the problems of the community they serve or to imagine their solution. If such institutions were controlled by and accountable to the community, the belief runs, they would be more effectively, or at least more sensitively, run. A ghetto community school board would hire teachers who believed in the capacity of black children to learn; it would revamp the curriculum to make it more relevant, and would assign books about black city children rather than about Dick and Jane in their suburban house. The result would be more learning. A ghetto community health board would find ways to reduce waiting times in clinics, hire personnel who did not patronize or insult patients, provide health instruction in the patient's own language. The result would be more effective health care. Moreover, community control of social action programs is also seen as a means of developing self-reliance in the community itself—feelings of competence and confidence and political power that will release energies and reduce despair.

At the moment, the movement for community control focuses on the process of gaining power. The vocal advocates of community control of schools and other social services feel that much of the problem lies in the negativism and hostility of the people who now run these institutions. Once the community assumed control, it could hold the managers accountable in some sense, fire those with hostile attitudes, and significantly improve the level of service. Community control advocates have not yet focused on new methods or organization, nor do they support experimentation or systematic testing of new models. On the contrary, one senses among ghetto militants a deep antagonism to experimentation, which is often viewed as an instrument of establishment control. "We do not want our children used as guinea pigs" typifies the attitude.

The word "accountability" is used frequently but vaguely by the advocates of community control. One searches the literature and the conversations in vain to learn what accounts are to be rendered and to whom, or how a community will know that its own administrators are doing a better job. So far, only limited attention has been paid to specific performance measures and that only with the view to dramatizing how bad the situation is. In the District of Columbia, for example, Julius W. Hobson induced the school system to publish reading scores by school in an effort to prove to the community that ghetto schools were not teaching children to read.

The vagueness about accountability seems likely to be temporary. If community control in big-city school systems, for example, becomes a reality, two things will probably happen. First, the community and its representatives will have to face up to the question: Now that we have control what shall we do?

They will begin to search for proven models of more effective education, to demand the results of systematic experimentation. Second, improved measures of school performance will be called for. After all, no community can run a school directly. It has to elect a board, to appoint managers and teachers. Factions will develop and, along with them, disagreements about how well the school is being managed. One would expect a demand for performance measures to support one position or another, as well as community interest in test score changes, attendance rates, job and college placements, and, eventually, more subtle measures of student development and enthusiasm. But beyond this, there is almost certain to be a demand for performance measures from higher levels of government. In fact, development of reliable criteria may be the only condition on which states and cities will be willing to relinquish control to community boards and still pay the bills from the general tax system.

Those who favor community control of schools in cities, for example, are not arguing for financing schools out of neighborhood tax revenues. Even if it were practical to collect taxes at a neighborhood level, it would not be desirable to finance schools this way. Areas with low tax collections would often turn out to have high educational needs and vice versa. Ghetto areas with high concentrations of poor children would not have the resources necessary to support even average schools, let alone the more intensive and expensive education these children need. Clearly, school expenditures have to be redistributed in accordance with educational need if poor children are to have a chance at equal education.

But the general city taxpayer is likely to have little enthusiasm for turning over funds to community or neighborhood boards without some assurance that he will get his money's worth. The community board will have to be in some sense accountable to the central treasury as well as to the members of the community itself. At a minimum, city-wide rules to protect the health and safety of school children will have to be devised. Beyond this, accounts might be rendered in terms of either inputs or outputs. Input rules governing the qualifications of teachers, the hiring and firing of personnel, the duties of teachers, the size of classes, will be favored by teachers' unions. But these are exactly the kinds of rules that brought about the demand for community control in the first place. Community groups may well argue for shifting to an output or performance measure in rendering their accounts to the city taxpayer, on these grounds: If the children learn, why do you care how we do it? This approach would necessitate the development of test scores and other types of performance measures acceptable both to community boards and to the city administration. In order to retain their right to operate the schools, community boards might be required to meet certain minimum performance standards. In addition, part of the school budget might be used to reward better-than-expected gains in performance measures.

The New York City Board of Education and the Educational Testing Service are designing a system to measure the effectiveness of the city's teachers and supervisors and to make them accountable. Such a system might even help reconcile the United Federation of Teachers with the devotees of community control.[4]

The Market Model

The market model is essentially an extreme form of decentralization. It moves the locus of decisions about how services should

4. See *New York Times*, Feb. 9, 1971.

be produced not simply to the community, but to the individual consumer.

The private sector of the economy relies on the profit motive to bring about improvement in the quality of goods and services offered to the consumer. If businesses want to survive, they have to attract customers by offering better products or lower prices than their competitors'—or both. The sanctions of the system are drastic: If the seller fails to produce what consumers want, he goes out of business. Success is also well rewarded. The firm that makes a "better" can opener or typewriter or lipstick can make millions.

Even economists know that this model does not work perfectly in the private sector. Sometimes there are too few sellers. They collude, overtly or tacitly. They may make profits—jointly—but the consumer loses. Antitrust laws and utility regulation exist to protect consumers against monopoly and oligopoly, but nobody really believes these laws and regulations work very effectively.

Moreover, even—or perhaps especially—when there are many sellers in the market, the level of public dissatisfaction with privately produced services can be high. Television and appliance repair, automobile servicing, laundering and dry cleaning are hardly objects of general consumer enthusiasm, even though they are privately produced by large numbers of competing sellers. True, the dissatisfied consumer can try another laundry, but he has little information to go on and may find the next place just as unsatisfactory as the last.

Despite these problems, some people believe that social services would be produced more effectively by private firms seeking to make a profit by pleasing the consumer. The argument is most frequently heard with respect to education. It runs thus: Children have to go to school and, in general, they have to go to the particular school in their neighborhood. Given this captive clientele, the school faculty and administration have little incentive to produce the kind of education that children and their parents want. The school management does not make money by producing more effective education, and nobody puts the school system out of business if the children fail to learn.

These observations have led some school reformers to the position that the only way to get effective education is to break the monopoly of public schools. They would not abolish public support of education, but they would channel it through the consumer rather than the producer.[5] Vouchers would entitle parents to buy education at whatever private or public school they found best for their children.

The voucher idea has attracted a spectrum of proponents that runs from the conservative economist Milton Friedman to liberal writer Christopher S. Jencks. Friedman's proposal was a simple one:

> . . . Governments would continue to administer some schools but parents who chose to send their children to other schools would be paid a sum equal to the estimated cost of educating a child in a government school, provided that at least this sum was spent on education in an approved school.[6]

The plan devised by a team headed by Jencks was a more complex proposal designed to meet some of the objections to the Friedman scheme.[7]

5. *Harvard Educational Review*, Vol. 38 (Winter 1968), devoted to equal educational opportunity, includes several articles on this subject. See also Theodore R. Sizer, "The Case for a Free Market," *Saturday Review*, Vol. 52 (Jan. 11, 1969), beg. p. 34

6. Milton Friedman, "The Role of Government in Education," in Robert A. Solo (ed.), *Economics and the Public Interest* (Rutgers University Press, 1955), p. 130.

7. The plan is described in Center for the Study of Public Policy, "Financing Education by Grants to Parents, A Preliminary Report," prepared for the Office of Economic Opportunity (The Center, March 1970), pp. 50–58.

At the same time that they appealed to southern conservatives eager to escape public school integration, vouchers have also been seen as a way of improving the education of black children in the urban ghetto.[8] The proponents believe that a variety of private schools would spring up in and around the ghetto, many run by blacks for blacks. Since they would compete for students, schools that did not provide attractive facilities, relevant curricula, and teachers who believed in ghetto children and knew how to "turn them on" would not attract students. Many would try, but only those who gave the consumers what they wanted would survive. Ghetto parents, it is argued, want effective education for their children and will, with practice, know when they have found it.

One serious objection to a voucher system is that it might accentuate existing problems of income inequality.[9] Even if families received vouchers of the same value for each school-age child, schools offering more expensive education to those willing to pay a premium in addition to the voucher are likely to spring up. If experience is any guide, middle- and upper-income families will spend additional sums for what they believe to be superior education. After all, they do this now; some send their children to private schools and a great many more spend money on music lessons, summer camps, or "educational" family trips.

The result of an equal-size voucher system might well be expensive schools in the suburbs offering richer curricula, smaller classes, and more elaborate facilities to the children of the well-heeled, while the poor continued to study outmoded

8. Christopher Jencks, "Private Schools for Black Children," *New York Times Magazine*, Nov. 3, 1968, Sec. 6, beg. p. 30.

9. For a good critique of voucher plans, see Henry M. Levin, "The Failure of the Public Schools and the Free Market Remedy," *Urban Review*, Vol. 2 (June 1968), pp. 32–37 (Brookings Reprint 148).

material in crowded classrooms in dismal schools. The suburban schools would be able to pay higher salaries and attract better teachers. Even if inner-city children were not discriminated against through entrance requirements, they would be effectively barred by higher tuition and the cost of commuting.

It would be possible, of course, to give larger vouchers to poor children on the grounds that their educational needs are greater. The differentials would have to be very large, however, to compensate for *both* the disposition of well-to-do families to spend more than their voucher and the greater real costs of teaching low-income children effectively. Such steep differentials in favor of the poor might be politically less palatable to the electorate than more subtle forms of income redistribution.

Under Jencks's proposal, the value of the voucher to the school would vary inversely with the family income of the student, and schools participating in the system would be prohibited from charging tuition beyond the voucher. Thus schools would have an incentive to enroll low-income children. The more expensive private schools would either have to cut their budgets or cater only to those rich enough to forgo the voucher and pay the full costs themselves. This may sound attractive on paper, but one wonders about the political saleability of a plan that would allow parents to shop around for the "best" school, but prohibit them from spending any additional funds on their children's education.

The other major problem with the voucher system is consumer ignorance. Unless he knows what he is buying, a consumer cannot choose rationally. Yet, in the social action area, it is very difficult for him to find out anything about the quality of a service before he uses it. Moreover, the costs of shopping around or sampling the merchandise of a hospital or a school may be prohibitive. In the medical area, they are obviously disastrous; one cannot shop around for a surgeon. But even in education, trial and error may be very costly. Parents cannot move a child around from one school to another until they find one they like, without endangering the child's educational and social progress. Moreover, even educated parents have trouble judging whether their child is progressing as rapidly as he could in school. How much greater, then, are the barriers to accurate parental judgment in the ghetto, where parents have little experience with books and learning.

If a voucher system is to increase the effectiveness of education, performance measures will have to be developed and made available so that parents can judge how much progress their children are making in school and how much they might make if they went to a different school. Hardly any schools, even private schools, provide anything resembling performance measures now. At best, a family considering alternative high schools may be able to find out where last year's graduates went to college, but this tells them little about the performance of the school. If a high proportion of graduates go to very selective colleges, it may mean only that the school tends to attract able and highly motivated students.

What kind of measures should schools produce for the information of current and potential consumers? First, a variety of measures, reflecting various objectives of education, should be developed and published. Publication of reading scores, for example, would prompt many parents to ask for evidence of other accomplishments, which might be poorly correlated with reading. What about mathematics and other cognitive skills? What about general ability to reason and oral expression and ability to get along with other children? What about leadership training and athletics and citizenship? Eventually, a variety of measures should be developed, validated, and published so that students and parents can choose intelligently among schools emphasizing the objectives of education they value most.

Second, to be useful, the measures have to reflect change in the student's performance over time rather than absolute levels of achievement. The absolute levels tell nothing about the effectiveness of the school. High reading scores may reflect only a student body selected for intelligence or verbal facility. The family of a child with a learning problem might well want to select a school with low absolute scores but higher rates of change at that level.

These two criteria raise the specter of constant testing and measurement, and of concentration on measurable skills to the detriment of the more subtle values of education. These are real dangers, but without serious effort to improve measures of education performance and to make them available, it is hard to see how a voucher system can lead to intelligent consumer choice and consumer pressure for effective education.

Moreover, reliance on the market would strengthen, not weaken, the case for public subsidy of research in education and systematic testing of new methods. Individual schools fighting for survival in the marketplace could not take risks with unproved methods or undertake expensive development of new curricula or approaches; nor could market competitors be expected to band together for systematic testing of innovations. Indeed, an atomistic private market for education might produce even less innovation than we have now. In general, in the normally private sectors of the economy, rapid technological change and increases in productivity occur in the large-firm, monopolized industries, not in those characterized by many sellers and intense interfirm competition.

Perhaps major national manufacturers would invest considerable sums in new educational techniques, hoping that they could be proved more effective and then sold to schools seeking to enhance their attractiveness to students. These companies, however, would tend to invest in hardware and materials on which they could retain exclusive rights through patents and copyrights. There might be serious neglect of methods and approaches that, while conceivably more effective than hardware, could be easily copied without compensation to the original developer. For this reason, public as well as corporate investment in research and systematic testing of education methods would be necessary.

To sum up, experiments with market mechanisms in education are worth trying; indeed, the Office of Economic Opportunity has announced that it intends to experiment with voucher systems in a number of communities.[10] Nevertheless, the system has serious problems. It may not be possible to design a system that reduces rather than accentuates the differential between educational opportunities for the rich and the poor. Moreover, the problem of accountability remains. If the taxpayer is to provide subsidies for education, he must have some assurance that the money is not wasted, that some minimum standards are met by institutions cashing in the voucher. Beyond these considerations, the system will not work as intended to increase educational effectiveness unless performance measures are developed so that the consumer can choose intelligently, and unless an organized public effort is made to develop and test new and improved methods.

Where Do We Go from Here?

The point of the above discussion is that all the likely scenarios for improving the effectiveness of education, health, and other

10. Fred M. Hechinger, "School Vouchers: Can the Plan Work?" *New York Times*, June 7, 1970; Eric Wentworth, "OEO Plans Test of Education Vouchers," *Washington Post*, Dec. 26, 1970.

social services dramatize the need for better performance measures. No matter who makes the decisions, effective functioning of the system depends on measures of achievement. If federal, state, or city governments manage social service delivery directly, they need ways to gauge the success of different methods of delivering services so that they can choose the best ones. If social service management is decentralized, or even turned over to communities, both the community and higher levels of government will need performance measures on the basis of which to identify and reward more effective management. Even if social services are turned over to the private market in hope of harnessing competition and the profit motive to improvements in performance, consumers, to make wise choices, will need measures of what they are buying or might buy.

It therefore seems to me that analysts who want to help improve social service delivery should give high priority to developing and refining measures of performance. Relatively little effort has gone into devising such measures so far, despite their importance and the apparent intellectual challenge of the task. In education it will be necessary to move beyond standardized tests to more sensitive and less culturally biased measures that reflect not only the intellectual skills of children, but their creativity and faith in themselves and enthusiasm for learning. In health, it will be necessary to move beyond the conventional mortality and hospitalization statistics to more refined measures of health and vigor. Poverty cannot be measured by income alone. Job satisfaction is probably not closely related to earnings or hours of work. Considerable imagination will have to be brought to bear before performance measures can be developed for services like counseling and psychiatric care.

Two general rules can be suggested for the development of

performance measures in the social action area. First, *single measures of social service performance should be avoided.* They will always lead to distortion, stultification, cheating to "beat the system," and other undesirable results. Schools cannot be judged by reading scores alone or mathematics scores alone or college placements alone or retention rates alone. Health service systems cannot be judged simply and solely by the number of patients treated or by the number of patients cured or even by health problems prevented. Manpower training programs cannot be weighed only by job placements or job retention or wage levels. Judging schools by reading scores would mean neglect of other skills and other dimensions of child development; judging a health center by the number of patients treated would encourage assembly line medicine; judging a manpower program on job placements would lead to hasty placement of trainees in low-level or unsuitable jobs.

Multiple measures are necessary to reflect multiple objectives and to avoid distorting performance. One can imagine schools developing and publishing a variety of measures of skills, knowledge, and satisfaction of students, some immediate and some based on longer-term follow-up. One can imagine health programs developing a variety of measures of health status and satisfaction of patients, also with different time lags. One can imagine manpower programs developing a variety of measures of skills acquired and subsequent job success of trainees.

For some purposes measures without any weights would be sufficient. In a voucher system for education, for example, one could simply make available a variety of performance measures for each school and let parents and students choose among them according to their own weighting systems. On the other hand, in a federal grant program designed to encourage effective manpower training, it would be necessary to assign weights to the various success measures being used. If several are being combined, the weights may not much matter, as long as no one measure is allowed to dominate and distort the reward system.

Second, *performance measures must reflect the difficulty of the problem.* If absolute levels of performance are rewarded, then schools will select the brightest students, training programs will admit only the workers who will be easiest to place in jobs, health centers will turn away or neglect the hopelessly ill. To avoid these distortions, social service effectiveness must always be measured in relation to the difficulty of the task. In general, measures of change are better than measures of absolute level, but even this approach may not solve the problem. It may be easier to bring about significant changes in the performance of bright children than in that of retarded children or to improve the health status of certain classes of patients. In this situation, the success of a social action activity can be measured only in relation to success of other activities with the same kind of student or patient or trainee. A considerable period of time will be necessary to collect experience and delineate above- and below-average performance with particular types of problems.

None of this sounds easy to accomplish. And it isn't. Nevertheless, we are unlikely to get improved social services (or, indeed, to know if we have them) until we make a sustained effort to develop performance measures suitable for judging and rewarding effectiveness. Current efforts to publish test scores or infant mortality rates in the name of "assessment" or "accountability" are only the first halting steps on the long road to better social services.

Performance measures for social services are not, of course, ends in themselves. They are prerequisites to attempts both to find more effective methods of delivering social services and to construct incentives that will encourage their use. But all the strategies for finding better methods discussed in these pages, especially social experimentation, depend for their success on improving performance measures. So do all the models for better incentives. Put more simply, to do better, we must have a way of distinguishing better from worse.

Index

Aged: public assistance for, 17
Aid for Families with Dependent Children (AFDC): family assistance plan effect, 30; inadequacies of, 17–18

Bank Street College of Education: Follow Through program, 104
Barber, Bernard, 109*n*
Bateman, Worth, 26*n*, 129*n*
Becker, Gary, 38*n*
Becker-Engelmann program: Follow Through program, 103–04
Behavior models: need for, in systematic analysis, 32–35, 45
Benefit-cost analysis: disease control study, 53–54; in investment programs, 60–63; manpower training study, 54; methods in, 51–53, 55–56; political process variable, 58–60; weaknesses in, 56–60
Berls, Robert H., 79*n*
Blind: public assistance for, 17
Bowden, D. Lee, 101*n*
Bowles, Samuel S., 71*n*, 72
Burkhead, Jesse, 71, 73, 74*n*
Bushell program: Follow Through program, 104

Campbell, Donald T., 111
Carnegie Commission on Higher Education, 44
Chase, Samuel B., Jr., 52*n*
Children: AFDC program for, 17–18; children's allowance proposals, 22–24, 27–28; family assistance plan proposals, 30
Cohen, David K., 105*n*
Cohen, Wilbur J., 20, 26–27
Coleman, James S., 13*n*, 71*n*
Coleman, John R., 56, 57*n*
Coleman report, 13, 71, 77
Community action programs: as random innovation strategy, 88
Community control proposals: government role, 132–33; performance incentives, 131–33
Computer technology: attitudes toward, 4; privacy factor, 15; survey use, 9, 15
Connery, Robert H., 43*n*
Cooper, Mildred P., 77*n*
Cort, H. R., Jr., 77*n*
Council of Economic Advisers, 10–11

Decentralization proposals: accountability mechanisms, 126–29; attitudes toward, 123–24; federal role, 125–27
Decision-making process: acceptance of PPBS, 1–5; *see also* Systematic analysis
Denison, Edward F., 41
Disabled: public assistance for, 17
Dorfman, Robert, 52*n*

Education, elementary and secondary: benefit-cost studies, 55–56; Coleman report, 12–13, 71, 77; community control proposals, 130–33; Follow Through program, 102–06; input-output studies, 69–78; longitudinal analysis need, 77–78; objectives in, 48–50; performance contracting, 106–08; performance measures in, 13, 121, 129, 138–40; resource-performance ratio, 73–74; socioeconomic variable, 13, 72; systematic experimentation in, 92–93; test inadequacies, 69–70, 75, 82–83; voucher system, 106, 109, 135–40
Education, higher: benefit-cost studies, 38–42; data inadequacies on, 78–79; equality of opportunity for, 37–45; financial crisis in, 36–37; studies of, 42–45
Educational Testing Service, 133
Egbert, Robert L., 104*n*
Elementary and Secondary Education Act of *1965*, 12, 23; analysis of Title I, 80–84; as random innovation strategy, 88–89; Title III, 88

Family assistance plan, 16; benefit-cost studies for, 28–29, 33–34; effect on existing welfare programs, 29–30; work incentive in, 29–31
Flanagan, John C., 13*n*, 71*n*
Follow Through program, 102–06
Fox, Thomas G., 71*n*
Friedman, Milton, 22*n*, 135

Gaither, H. Rowan, 1
Gorham, William, 92, 93*n*
Green, Christopher, 22*n*, 25*n*
Gross, Bertram M., 47*n*
Guthrie, James W., 73

Hansen, W. Lee, 38*n*, 40, 71*n*
Hartman, Robert W., 41*n*
Hauser, Gerald, 35*n*
Hawthorne effect, 89, 89*n*–90*n*, 116
Headstart program, 84–85, 102–03, 118
Health: disease control study, 53–54; medicaid, 23–24, 67; medicare, 23–24, 67; performance measures, 121; survey data need, 14–15, 48; systematic experimentation, need for, 91–92
Health, Education, and Welfare, Department of (HEW), 2; budget constraints, 23–25; decision process in, 5–6; income maintenance studies, 24–27; *Toward a Social Report*, 47–48
Hechinger, Fred M., 140*n*
Heineman Commission, 34
Higher Education Act of *1965*, 23
Hildebrand, George H., 22*n*
Hitch, Charles J., 1–2, 4*n*
Hobson, Julius W., 131
Holland, John W., 71*n*

Income maintenance: behavioral studies need, 34–35, 102; benefit-cost studies, 28–29, 32–34; budget constraints, 23–25; children's allowance proposals, 22–24, 27; current system of, 16–19; data inadequacies, 19; family assistance plan, 27–31; federal floor proposals, 20–21, 26–27; negative income tax proposals, 21–22, 25–26, 96–100; New Jersey Graduated Work Incentive Experiment in, 94–102; *see also* Welfare

Jencks, Christopher S., 135, 136*n*, 137
Johnson, Lyndon Baines, 14, 27, 42
Judgment: in decision-making process, 2

Katzman, Martin T., 49*n*
Kelly, James F., 19*n*
Kelly, Terence F., 101*n*
Kershaw, Joseph, 22
Kiesling, Herbert J., 71

Labor, Department of, 2
Lampman, Robert J., 22*n*
Language: educational testing factor, 48
Levin, Henry M., 72, 74*n*, 136*n*
Levine, Robert A., 22, 124
Lindblom, Charles E., 1
Lyday, James M., 26*n*

Man-in-the-house rule, 17–18, 18*n*–19*n*, 20
Manpower training: benefit-cost analysis of, 54; performance measures, 127–29
Market model proposals: theory of, 133–35; voucher education, 135–40
Mayeske, George W., 71
McClung, Nelson, 11*n*
Medicaid, 23–24, 67
Medicare, 23–24, 67
Medicine, *see* Health
Meyer, Philip, 83*n*
Mieszkowski, Peter M., 22*n*, 96*n*
Migration: welfare differential as factor in, 18–19, 95
Milius, Peter, 83*n*
Model cities program: as random innovation strategy, 88
Moeller, John, 11*n*
Moore, Wilbert E., 47*n*
Mosback, E. J., 81*n*
Moynihan, Daniel P., 27
Mundel, David S., 41

Nathan, Richard, 27

National Assessment of Education, 49
National Welfare Rights Organization, 34
Negative income tax: New Jersey Graduated Work Incentives Experiment, 96–100; proposals for, 21–22, 25–26, 29; *see also* Income maintenance
Neighborhood Youth Corps (NYC), 112
New Jersey Graduated Work Incentive Experiment: design, 97–100; reasons for, 94–97; results, 100–02
Nixon, Richard M., 16, 31, 65, 100

Office of Economic Opportunity (OEO), 2, 85, 124; budget, 23; Follow Through program, 102–03; income maintenance experiment, 94–102; negative income tax proposals, 22
Office of Education: Follow Through program, 103–04; Texarkana project, 107–08
Okner, Benjamin A., 11*n*, 35*n*
Olson, Mancur, 47*n*
O'Neill, June, 43*n*
Orcutt, Alice G., 97*n*
Orcutt, Guy H., 97*n*
Orshansky, Mollie, 17*n*

Peacock, Alan T., 35*n*
Pechman, Joseph A., 22*n*, 35*n*, 40, 96*n*
Performance contracting: in education, 106–08
Performance measures: in community control proposals, 130–33; in education, 13, 121, 129, 138–40; in decentralization proposals, 122–30; in market system proposals, 133–40; in manpower training, 127–29; need for effective, 120–22, 141–44
Planning-programming-budgeting system (PPBS), acceptance of, 1–6; *see also* Systematic analysis; Systematic experimentation
Poverty: definitions of, 11–12, 17; myths of, 11–12; Survey of Economic Opportunity, 10–11, 29, 33; *see also* Income maintenance; Welfare
President's Commission on Income Maintenance Programs, *see* Heineman Commission
Privacy: computer data and, 15
Project TALENT, 13*n*, 39, 71, 77
Public assistance programs, 17–19

Random innovation: strategy of, 87–91
Random selection process: in systematic experimentation, 111–12
Ribich, Thomas I., 55, 58, 71
Rosen, Ronald S., 49*n*

Schorr, Alvin, 23
Schultze, Charles L., 1, 24*n*, 58*n*, 120, 121*n*

Shaycoft, Marion F., 71
Sheldon, Eleanor B., 47*n*
Siguel, Eduardo, 11*n*
Sills, David L., 90*n*
Singer, Leslie, 101*n*
Sizer, Theodore R., 135*n*
Social Security Administration, 11–12, 17
Solo, Robert A., 135*n*
Somers, Gerald G., 112*n*
Spiegelman, Robert, 101*n*
Stanford Research Institute, 105
Stromsdorfer, Ernst W., 112*n*
Survey of Economic Opportunity (SEO), 10–11, 29, 33
Survey of Educational Opportunity, *see* Coleman report
Survey techniques: accuracy of, 11–12; census, 9–10; in education studies, 12–13; in health studies, 14–15, 48; inadequacies, 15, 34–35; in income maintenance studies, 31–35; Survey of Economic Opportunity (SEO), 10–11, 29, 33; U.S. National Health Survey, 14
Systematic analysis: acceptance of, 4–6; benefit-cost studies, 51–63; of education, 38–45, 69–70, 74–78; of income maintenance, 31–35; need for, 141–44
Systematic experimentation: arguments for, 109; description of, 91; in education, 92–93; ethics of, 109–11; federal role, 92–93; Follow Through program, 102–06; Hawthorne effect in, 116; honesty in, 112–14; New Jersey Graduated Work Incentive Experiment, 94–102; political use of, 113; random selection in, 111–12; technical problems in, 114–19

Tax model, 35–36
TEMPO: Title I study, 81–83
Tobin, James, 22*n*, 96*n*

United Federation of Teachers, 133
U.S. National Health Survey, 14

Values: in decision-making process, 2
Voucher system: in education, 106, 109, 135–40

Watts, Harold W., 99*n*, 100*n*, 101
Weisbrod, Burton A., 40, 58–59
Welfare: AFDC, 17–18; children's allowance proposals, 22–24, 27–28; current, 16–19; eligibility requirements, 18, 20; family assistance plan proposal, 16, 27–31, 33–34; federalization proposals, 20–21, 26–27; negative income tax proposals, 20–21, 25–26; *see also* Income maintenance
Wholey, Joseph S., 14*n*
Wiley, George, 34
Willcox, Alanson W., 110*n*

Williams, Walter, 26*n*
Wolk, Ronald A., 36*n*
Work Experience and Training Program in HEW, 129
Work incentive: in family assistance plan, 28–31; negative income tax proposals, 21; New Jersey Graduated Work Incentive Experiment, 94–102; WIN program, 62

Southern Methodist Univ.
3 2177 01451 6213